S0-AWK-408

Pillsbury's Bake Off Breads Cook Book

Showcased favorites... the best of all the Bake Offs, streamlined for ease with new instant dry yeast

Dear Homemaker,

Creatively speaking, bread is the most rewarding kind of food a woman can prepare. Something magic happens to dough in the oven that creates a great satisfaction. You'll feel the warm appreciation from your family and guests for offering them the homey goodness of breads, rolls or snacks you baked yourself.

In this book, we have selected the best of the breads and snacks from eighteen years of Pillsbury Bake Offs, and brought them up to date using today's easy methods of bread preparation and convenient prepared foods. You'll find all the yeast bread recipes use the easy no-dissolve method of preparation, where the yeast is mixed directly with the flour.

The hundred and eighty-seven recipes in this book range from aromatic yeast breads and quick breads to sensational snacks. Each recipe is described and given a "start-to-finish" time, but remember, only about a quarter of the given time is spent in actual preparation.

We hope these recipes encourage you to become one of those esteemed homemakers about whom it is whispered, "She bakes her own breads!"

Cordially yours,

Ann Pillsbury

Copyright © 1968 by the Pillsbury Company. Printed in U.S.A.

Contents

4 . . . Basics

8 . . . Terms

10 . . . Measures

12 . . . Frostings & Glazes

14 . . . Spreads

16 . . . New Method of Bread Making

21 . . . Yeast Breads

22 . . . Shaping a Loaf

39 . . . Dinner & Luncheon Rolls

40 . . . Shaping Rolls

55 . . . Batter Breads & Rolls

65 . . . Coffeetime Breads & Rolls

103 . . . Quick Breads

125 . . . Snacks

Basics

. . . **Flour** is the major ingredient in bread, forming the structural framework. Because flours vary in the combination of soft and hard wheat, a range of flour is given with most recipes. The softer wheat flours have less moisture-absorbing capacity, thus requiring more flour to form a stiff dough. Temperature and humidity changes affect the amount of flour necessary — more flour is needed on humid days to produce a dough which is easily handled.

Pillsbury's Best All Purpose Flour and Pillsbury's Best Self-Rising Flour have been used in developing the recipes used in this book. When measuring either all purpose or self-rising flour, there is no need to sift flour; measure by lightly spooning into cup, and then leveling off with the straight edge of a spatula or knife. The self-rising flour has added leavenings and salt and is made from a softer wheat. Thus, it is sometimes necessary to increase the amount of self-rising flour added.

. . . **Yeast** is a living plant that makes yeast breads rise and gives the light, porous structure. Yeast is temperature-sensitive — too hot a temperature kills the yeast, too cold retards growth.

Yeast is available in active dry and compressed forms. Active dry yeast has been used in developing the recipes in this book. Two sizes of active dry yeast are available — individual packages and vacuum-packed jars. One package ($^3/_5$ oz.) compressed yeast may be softened and substituted for one package active dry yeast. The active dry yeast may be stored at room temperature. However, compressed yeast must be stored in the refrigerator. Check expiration date on the yeast package.

Basics continued

... **Sugar** adds flavor, gives a golden crust and provides food for the yeast. Increasing the amount of sugar hastens rising, but too much retards growth. Sugar is particularly necessary in refrigerated dough to provide food for the yeast.

... **Salt** is used primarily for flavor. It also helps strengthen the structural framework. Too much salt retards yeast growth resulting in compact, coarse breads.

... **Shortening, butter or margarine** give a tender, rich bread and improve browning. Many recipes in this book call for butter or margarine where either will work; however, butter adds a special flavor and richness. When a recipe calls for butter or margarine, softened, be sure it is warmed to room temperature in order to blend in with the other ingredients.

Special adjustments must be made when using whipped butter or margarine in cooking and baking. Whipped margarine has 6 sticks per pound instead of the usual 4. Thus, each stick has only ⅓ cup for recipe use instead of the usual ½ cup.

... **Liquid** is essential to combine with the flour to form the structural framework. Water, whole milk, skim milk or reconstituted nonfat dry milk may be used as the liquid. Water gives a hard, crisp crust and open texture similar to French breads. Milk gives a more nutritious, tender, flavorful bread that browns slightly better.

... **Eggs** add richness in flavor and color, resulting in a bread of finer, more delicate texture. Eggs should be stored in your refrigerator as they deteriorate rapidly at room temperatures. Buy eggs that have been refrigerated. Leftover egg whites and yolks can be stored in the refrigerator, tightly covered, for several days. If you wish to store them for a longer period, cover tightly and freeze, then thaw in the refrigerator. Remember that:

I egg white = *3 tablespoons*
I egg yolk = *I tablespoon*
I egg = *¼ cup*

. . . **Proofing** — Yeast breads and rolls are placed in a warm place (80° to 85° F.) to activate the yeast, causing the bread to rise or proof. There are several ways of providing a warm place for your bread to rise. One method is to turn on the oven at 400° for a minute. Then, turn off the oven and place the bowl of bread dough on the center oven rack, oven door closed. Another way of warming the oven is to place a large pan of hot water on the lowest oven rack, changing water as necessary. Or, if oven is not available, set the bowl of dough on top of the warm oven or in another warm place.

Since proofing conditions vary, an estimation of time is given on all recipes. If you are delayed in shaping the dough, keep punching it down and set in cooler place. If the shaped dough is proofed too long, the bread may collapse during baking. If dough is not proofed long enough, a small, coarse bread will result.

. . . **High altitude adjustments** — Adjustments are made where necessary for baking at high altitudes. No adjustment is given with yeast breads, but they will rise faster.

. . . **Storage of breads** — Storing and freezing breads for later use will add variety to your meals. If a recipe makes more than you can use, freeze the extra for later use. With small families, it's a good idea to divide and freeze in one-meal portions. Bread should be cooled completely before wrapping. Be sure the wrap is moisture-vapor proof, and all the air is removed.

Yeast breads are best kept at room temperature tightly wrapped in plastic or foil. However, if the bread contains meat, it should be stored in the refrigerator. If you plan to serve a bread warm, store it in foil so that it can easily be reheated in a 325° oven for about 20 minutes.

. . . **Menu planning** — Let the bread or rolls, bring out the best in your meal. If serving a hearty, elegant meat dish, choose a simple warm dinner roll. If having a rich, creamy casserole dish, accent your main course with a crusty, crunchy roll. Bring out bland flavors by choosing a savory bread or roll, rich with herbs and seasonings. Create interest in the meal by varying different shapes — muffins with chicken and breadsticks with pork chops. For a buffet or brunch, feature a variety of shapes, flavors and colors. Freeze extra portions and serve at a later time.

Terms

Special helps for directions and ingredients used in this book.

Directions:

Batter bread . . . A no-knead yeast bread of a batter consistency that is dropped or spread into pan.

Beat . . . To vigorously mix.

Blend . . . To combine two or more ingredients.

Boil . . . To heat or cook until bubbles break the surface.

Brown . . . To make food brown by exposing to dry oven heat or browning in small amount of fat on top of range.

Brush . . . To moisten surface with pastry brush.

Canapé . . . Small piece of bread or pastry topped with meat, fish or cheese, served as an appetizer.

Chop . . . To cut into small pieces.

Chill . . . To place in refrigerator or other cool place until cold.

Combine . . . To mix two ingredients together.

Cool until lukewarm . . . To let stand until mixture feels moderately warm — neither hot nor cold.

Cream . . . To blend a fat with sugar until light and creamy.

Cube . . . To cut into small cubes.

Cut in . . . To use pastry blender, two knives or fork to distribute shortening through dry ingredients, leaving small particles.

Cut up . . . To cut into very small pieces.

Deep-fat fry . . . To cook food by completely immersing in hot fat.

Dice . . . To cut into very small cubes.

Dot . . . To scatter small particles (usually butter) over food.

Dough . . . A mixture of moistened flour and other ingredients, stiff enough to be kneaded or handled.

Drizzle . . . To pour or drizzle a thin mixture in a back and forth motion.

Flake . . . To break into small pieces, usually with a fork.

Flour . . . To cover surface with thin layer of flour.

Fold . . . To combine delicate ingredients (beaten egg whites or whipped cream) without air loss. Insert spatula down through the middle of mixture, across bottom, bring it up and "fold" over onto mixture. Continue until all is evenly mixed.

Frosting . . . A thick, yet spreadable mixture of sugar, butter and other ingredients; usually spread.

Fry . . . To cook in hot fat.

Glaze . . . To coat with a thin mixture.

Grate . . . To rub a food against a grater to form small particles.

Grease . . . To cover with a layer of shortening, usually to prevent sticking to pan.

Greased and floured . . . To cover with layer of shortening, then coat lightly with flour.

Greased on bottom only . . . To cover the bottom of pan with layer of shortening. Sides need to be left ungreased so food can cling as it rises and bakes.

Heat until warm . . . To place over medium heat until mixture feels moderately warm.

Hors d'oeuvre . . . Appetizer served hot or cold.

Jelly-roll fashion . . . To shape dough by rolling up a large rectangle, to form a "jelly-roll" shape.

Knead . . . To work dough by repeatedly stretching it with the hands, folding it over, and pressing it with knuckles or "heel" of the hand.

Mince . . . To chop very fine.

Mix . . . To combine two or more ingredients.

Pare or peel . . . To remove the outer covering of a fruit or vegetable.

Sauté . . . To cook in a small amount of fat in a skillet.

Shred . . . To tear or cut into thin strips.

Simmer . . . To heat or cook just below the boiling point.

Stir until dry ingredients are moistened . . . To blend only until dry particles are completely moistened, even though batter is lumpy.

Ingredients:

Almond paste . . . A paste made of finely ground blanched almonds and sugar.

Cake and pastry filling . . . A ready-to-use thick fruit or nut paste.

Fruit pie filling . . . Prepared fruit in thickened sauce — ready to use.

Clove of garlic . . . One section of the garlic bulb.

Prepared dried peel . . . Commercially prepared dried lemon or orange peel.

Cream, light . . . Cream used in cooking but not high enough in butterfat to whip (about 20% butterfat).

Cream, whipping . . . Heavy cream that thickens when whipped (about 30% butterfat).

Dairy sour cream . . . Cream that has been soured by use of cultures. Do not substitute sour half and half or imitation sour cream in baking as the fat level, which is important as shortening, is lower.

Half and half . . . Very light cream — half milk, half cream.

Eggs, slightly beaten . . . Beaten just to combine yolk and white.

Eggs, well beaten . . . Beaten until foamy and light, completely combined.

Condensed milk (sweetened) . . . Canned whole milk from which the water has been evaporated and sugar added.

Evaporated milk . . . Canned whole milk from which half the water has been evaporated.

Cooking oil . . . A liquid fat.

Shortening . . . A solid, yet pliable fat made from vegetable or vegetable and animal fats.

Confectioners' sugar . . . A fine, powdery sugar, also known as powdered sugar.

Brown sugar, granulated . . . Brown sugar processed to make granular. If used in recipes, follow label for substitution amounts.

Active dry yeast . . . Granulated, stays fresh on the cupboard shelf.

Compressed yeast . . . Cake form, stays fresh for several weeks in refrigerator.

Measures

3 teaspoons	=	1 tablespoon
16 tablespoons	=	1 cup
2 cups	=	1 pint
2 pints	=	1 quart
4 quarts	=	1 gallon
8 fl. oz.	=	1 cup
16 oz.	=	1 lb.

Equivalents

Food	Quantity	Yields
Almonds	4 oz.	1 cup diced roasted or 1 cup slivered
Apple	1 medium	1 cup chopped or 1 cup sliced
Candied fruit	8 oz.	1½ cups cut up
Candied peel	8 oz.	1½ cups
Cheese	¼ lb. (4 oz.)	1 cup shredded
Cheese, cream	3 oz.	⅓ cup
Crackers, graham	15	1 cup fine crumbs
Dates	1 lb.	2 cups cut up
Lemon	1 lemon	2 to 3 tablespoons juice; 2 to 3 teaspoons grated peel
Milk, evaporated	6 oz.	¾ cup
	14½ oz.	1⅔ cups
Milk, sweetened condensed	15½ oz.	1⅓ cups
Onion	1 medium	½ cup chopped
Orange	1 medium	¼ to ⅓ cup juice; 1 to 2 tablespoons grated peel
Peanuts	5 oz.	1 cup
Pecans	4¼ oz.	1 cup chopped
	3¾ oz.	1 cup halves
Potato	1 medium	1 cup cubed
Raisins, seedless	1 lb.	3 cups
Sugar, brown	1 lb.	2¼ cups firmly packed
Sugar, confectioners'	1 lb.	3½ cups
Walnuts	4½ oz.	1 cup chopped
	3½ oz.	1 cup halves
Yeast, compressed	1 oz. package	2 packages active dry
	2 oz. package	4 packages active dry

Substitutions

Buttermilk . . . I tablespoon vinegar plus milk to make I cup = I cup buttermilk or sour milk

Chives . . . I tablespoon freeze-dried or frozen chives = I tablespoon chopped fresh chives

Garlic . . . ⅛ teaspoon garlic powder or ½ teaspoon garlic salt = I medium clove of garlic

Herbs . . . I tablespoon fresh herbs = I teaspoon dried herbs.

**Lemon or
Orange peel** . . . I teaspoon prepared dried peel = I teaspoon fresh grated peel

Onion . . . I tablespoon instant minced onion = ¼ cup chopped fresh onion
I tablespoon dried onion flakes = ¼ cup chopped fresh onion
I tablespoon onion salt = ¼ cup chopped fresh onion

Parsley . . . I tablespoon dried parsley flakes = 3 tablespoons chopped fresh parsley

Yeast . . . I scant tablespoon active dry yeast = I package active dry yeast
I package active dry yeast = I cake (³/₅ oz.) compressed yeast

Can Sizes

Size	Weight	Approximate Cups
4 oz.	4 oz.	½ cup
8 oz.	8 oz.	I cup
Picnic	10½ to 12 oz.	1½ cups
12 oz. vacuum	12 oz.	1½ cups
#300	14 to 16 oz.	1¾ cups
#303	16 to 17 oz.	2 cups
#2	I lb. 4 oz. or I pt. 2 fl. oz.	2½ cups
#2½	I lb. 13 oz.	3½ cups
#3	3 lb. 3 oz. or I qt. 14 fl. oz.	5¾ cups
#10	6 lb. 8 oz. to 7 lb. 5 oz.	12 to 13 cups

Frostings & Glazes

• Add a special touch to your breads and rolls with a frosting or glaze. Pick a complimentary flavor; then spread with a creamy frosting or drizzle with a thin, shiny glaze. Top with a few nuts or fruit — the final touch to picture-perfect breads.

Frosting

1 cup confectioners' sugar
1 tablespoon butter or margarine, softened
1 to 2 tablespoons milk

Glaze

1 cup confectioners' sugar
2 to 3 tablespoons milk

In small mixing bowl, combine all ingredients; blend until smooth. Add more milk, a few drops at a time, until of spreading consistency or drizzling consistency.

Tip: Fruit juices may be substituted for milk; add food coloring if desired.

Vanilla
Add ½ teaspoon vanilla.

Almond
Add ¼ teaspoon almond extract.

Maple
Add ¼ teaspoon maple flavoring.

Orange or Lemon
Add ¼ teaspoon grated peel and substitute fruit juice for the milk.

Chocolate
Add 1 tablespoon cocoa or ½ square (½ oz.) unsweetened chocolate, melted.

Coffee
Add ½ teaspoon instant coffee.

Mocha
Add 1 tablespoon cocoa and ½ teaspoon instant coffee.

Spice
Add ¼ teaspoon cinnamon and dash of nutmeg.

Rum or Brandy
Add ¼ teaspoon rum or brandy flavoring, or 1 teaspoon rum or brandy.

<u>To Glaze:</u> *Glaze doughnuts by dipping and swirling in glaze just thick enough to thinly coat the surface. Let stand, glazed side up, on wire rack until set.*

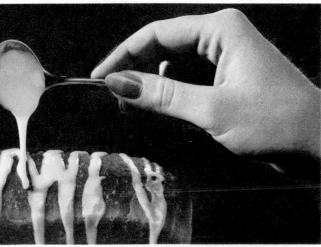

<u>To Drizzle:</u> *Glazes are thin enough to drizzle over the top of your coffee cake or bread in attractive patterns. Coffee cake should be cool enough so that glaze holds its shape.*

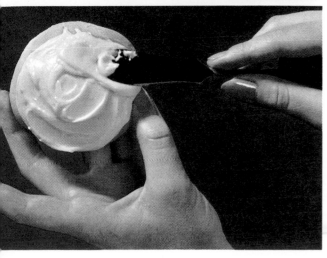

<u>To Spread:</u> *Frostings are creamy enough to spread easily without tearing bread. Most breads need only a thin layer of frosting to compliment their flavors.*

Spreads

• Dress up your breads with a special spread or topping! Pretty tea sandwiches look so elegant on your favorite tray. Use spreads and toppings for open-faced sandwiches or as fillings for fancy sandwiches. Cut out any shape, use any filling, then garnish with olives, candied fruit or nuts. Presto . . . fancy sandwiches awaiting your guests.

Whipped Butter (Light 'n fluffy with any bread . . . an easy gourmet touch)

   ½ cup butter, softened
   2 tablespoons milk or cream

In small mixer bowl, blend butter and milk. Beat until light and fluffy.

Honey Butter (An old favorite to go on any bread . . . particularly good on toasted English muffins)

   ½ cup butter, softened
   ½ cup honey

In small mixer bowl, blend butter and honey. Beat until light and fluffy.

Festive Olive Spread (Add color and zest to canapés or tea sandwiches with this festive spread)

   ½ cup butter, softened
   2 tablespoons milk or cream
   2 tablespoons thinly sliced
     stuffed green olives

In small mixer bowl, beat butter and milk until light and fluffy. Stir in olives.

Hard Sauce (Vanilla frosting mix whips into a rum-flavored spread, perfect on nut breads for the holidays)

   I package one layer size Pillsbury
     Buttercream Vanilla Frosting Mix
   ½ cup butter, softened
   I egg
   ½ teaspoon rum flavoring

In small mixer bowl, blend frosting mix with butter until smooth and creamy. Add egg and rum flavoring; beat until light and fluffy.

Cheese 'n Honey Topping (Add a touch of honey to your breads)

> 1 package (3 oz.) cream cheese
> ¼ cup honey

In small mixer bowl, beat cream cheese until light and fluffy. Gradually add honey, beating until well blended.

Cherry Cream Cheese Spread (Perfect for holiday fruit breads made into open-faced sandwiches)

> 1 package (3 oz.) cream cheese
> 1 tablespoon chopped maraschino cherries
> 1 teaspoon milk

In small mixer bowl, whip cream cheese and milk until fluffy. Fold in cherries.

Coffee Cream Cheese Spread (Fluffy coffee-flavored spread that adds a new twist to your favorite nut or raisin loaf)

> 2 packages (3 oz. each) cream cheese
> 1 egg yolk
> ¼ cup confectioners' sugar
> ¼ teaspoon instant coffee

In small mixer bowl, combine all ingredients. Beat until light and fluffy.

Fluffy Orange Spread (A nice compliment to any fruit or nut bread)

> 2 packages (3 oz. each) cream cheese
> ¼ cup orange juice
> 1 tablespoon sugar
> 1 tablespoon grated orange peel

In small mixer bowl, beat cream cheese and orange juice until smooth and creamy. Add sugar and orange peel, beating until well blended.

8 Views of the New of Bread Making

1 *"In large mixer bowl, combine part of flour, sugar, salt and dry yeast."*

By distributing the dry yeast throughout the dry ingredients, the yeast is more protected from extreme liquid temperatures. Only part of the flour is added — an amount about equal to the liquid measurement. If too much flour is added, the yeast will not dissolve completely and the mixture will be too stiff for beating on an electric mixer.

2 *"In saucepan, heat milk and shortening . . . . (Shortening does not need to melt.)"*

The milk should be heated until warm for proper yeast action. Chilled butter or margarine should be cut into pieces to allow to soften while milk is warming. If butter is not softened, it will be difficult to blend in and some lumps of butter may be seen in the dough. The milk should be moderately warm, not hot, when added to the flour-yeast mixture. If too hot, the milk may kill the yeast; if too cool, the yeast may not dissolve completely.

Method

• A new granulation in the active dry yeast now available makes possible this easy method of bread making. The dry yeast is combined with the other dry ingredients, omitting the need to soften in water. Recipes for yeast breads in this book use this easy method of preparation. If you prefer, you can still prepare the recipes in this book by dissolving the yeast, active dry or compressed, in warm water — ¼ cup for each package of yeast — and then add with other liquid. Count this water as part of the total liquid addition in the recipe. To help you become familiar with this new method, here are 8 views of the step by step preparation.

---

3 *"Add eggs and warm milk . . . Blend at low speed; beat at medium speed."*

Blending at low speed combines all the ingredients; beating at medium speed develops the flour structural framework, eliminating or reducing the kneading time.

4 *"By hand, stir in remaining flour to form a stiff dough."*

A range of flour is given to accommodate varying conditions such as humidity, temperature and softness of flour. Doughs that will be kneaded or shaped need enough flour to make the dough easy to handle.

Bread Making-
continued

5 *"Knead on floured surface until smooth and elastic."*

Rub enough flour into the surface so that the dough will not stick and can be handled easily. It may be necessary to add more flour as you knead. To knead, stretch dough by folding edges of dough in toward center, then press with knuckles or heel of hand. Repeat, turning dough one-quarter turn around.

6 *"Place in greased bowl, turning to grease top. Cover; . . . ."*

Place in a large enough bowl so dough will have room to double in size. Turning to grease top and covering with plastic wrap helps prevent crust formation during proofing.

7

"Let rise in warm place until light and doubled in size."

Yeast dough needs a warm place (80° to 85° F.) for rising. Proofing suggestions are given on page 7. The approximate time required for dough to double in size is given with each recipe. When dough is approximately doubled in size, a fingertip depression will remain.

8

"Punch down dough."

Punch down in center of dough with fist. This step removes large air bubbles so that your baked bread will be fine textured.

Yeast Breads

● The baking aroma of a good yeast bread can start hunger pangs quicker than anything we know. In this chapter you can choose from a gala parade of flavors and shapes . . . from peanut butter to caraway, from elegantly long French loaves to round ryes. Many use the mixer to shorten kneading time. Once out of the oven, cool them before slicing gently with a serrated knife or an electric knife, or cool, wrap and freeze for later use.

Shaping a Loaf

• When your bread dough is ready for shaping, follow these 6 easy step-by-step directions to picture-pretty loaves.

1 Divide dough into number of loaves specified in recipe. Roll out dough on floured surface to a 14x7-inch rectangle.

3 Pinch edges and ends to seal.

4 Place shaped loaf, seam-side down, in well-greased 9x5-inch loaf pan.

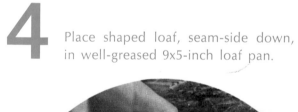

2 Starting with 7-inch side, roll up jelly-roll fashion, sealing well with heel of hand after each turn.

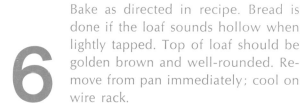

5 Cover; let rise in warm place until light and doubled in size.

6 Bake as directed in recipe. Bread is done if the loaf sounds hollow when lightly tapped. Top of loaf should be golden brown and well-rounded. Remove from pan immediately; cool on wire rack.

Good old fashioned rye bread with a hint of anise or caraway. The secret to its special moistness is buttermilk. Prepare in three and a half hours.

Scandinavian Rye Bread

　　3 cups rye flour
　⅓ cup firmly packed brown sugar
　　3 teaspoons salt
　　I tablespoon grated orange peel
　　I teaspoon anise seed
　½ teaspoon soda
　　2 packages active dry yeast
　　I cup buttermilk or sour milk
　¼ cup molasses
　¼ cup shortening
　　I cup warm water
　　3 to 3½ cups Pillsbury's Best All Purpose
　　　Flour*

OVEN 350°　　　　　　　　　　　　2 LOAVES

In large mixer bowl, combine rye flour, brown sugar, salt, orange peel, anise seed, soda and dry yeast. In saucepan, heat buttermilk, molasses and shortening until buttermilk is warm. (Shortening does not need to melt.) Add warm water and buttermilk mixture to rye flour mixture. Blend at lowest speed until moistened; beat 3 minutes at medium speed. By hand, stir in flour to form a stiff dough. Knead on floured surface until smooth and elastic, about 5 minutes. Place in greased bowl, turning to grease top. Cover; let rise in warm place until light and doubled in size, I to I½ hours.

Punch down dough. Shape into 2 round loaves. Place on opposite corners of greased cookie sheet. Cover; let rise in warm place until light and doubled in size, about I hour. Bake at 350° for 45 to 50 minutes until deep golden brown.

Tips: For a delicious caraway rye bread, substitute caraway seed for anise seed.

This can be shaped into two loaves and baked in greased 9x5-inch loaf pans as directed above.

*For use with Pillsbury's Best Self-Rising Flour, decrease salt to 2 teaspoons and omit soda.

Chewy dates and chopped nuts tucked into a rich, moist loaf husbands adore. Add a bright finish with sugar-orange glaze. Better made a day ahead.

Up-To-Date Bread

8 to 8½ cups Pillsbury's Best All Purpose
    Flour*
2 tablespoons sugar
3 teaspoons salt
2 packages active dry yeast
1½ cups cut-up dates
1 cup chopped nuts
3 cups milk
2 tablespoons shortening

Glaze

2 tablespoons orange juice
2 tablespoons sugar

OVEN 375°   3 LOAVES

In large mixing bowl, combine 4 cups of flour, sugar, salt, dry yeast, dates and nuts. In large saucepan, heat milk and shortening until milk is warm. (Shortening does not need to melt.) Add to dry ingredients; mix until well blended. Stir in remaining flour to form a stiff dough. Knead on well-floured surface until smooth and elastic, 5 to 10 minutes. Place in greased bowl, turning to grease top. Cover; let rise in warm place until light and doubled in size, 1½ to 2 hours.

Punch down dough; divide into 3 parts. Shape into loaves. Place in greased 9x5-inch loaf pans. Cover; let rise in warm place until light and doubled in size, 45 to 60 minutes. Bake at 375° for 40 to 45 minutes. Remove from pans immediately. Brush with Glaze, if desired.

Glaze: Combine orange juice and sugar; mix well.

*For use with Pillsbury's Best Self-Rising Flour, omit salt.

The nutty goodness of whole wheat is accented with honey; frosted with honey glaze, if desired. Allow five hours to make and bake.

Honey-Wheat Bread

3 cups whole wheat flour
½ cup honey
3 teaspoons salt
1 package active dry yeast
1 cup milk
2 tablespoons shortening
1 cup warm water
3 to 3½ cups Pillsbury's Best All Purpose
    Flour*

Honey Glaze

1 cup confectioners' sugar
¼ cup chopped pecans
1 tablespoon honey
2 to 3 tablespoons milk

OVEN 350°   2 LOAVES

In large mixer bowl, combine whole wheat flour, honey, salt and dry yeast. In saucepan, heat milk and shortening until milk is warm. (Shortening does not need to melt.) Add warm milk and water to flour mixture. Blend at lowest speed until moistened; beat 3 minutes at medium speed. By hand, stir in all purpose flour to form a stiff dough. Knead on floured surface until smooth and elastic, about 5 minutes. Place in greased bowl, turning to grease top. Cover; let rise in warm place until light and doubled in size, 1 to 1½ hours.

Punch down dough; divide in half. Shape into two loaves and place in two well-greased 9x5-inch loaf pans. Cover; let rise in warm place until light and doubled in size, 1½ to 2 hours. Bake at 350° for 50 to 60 minutes until golden brown. Cool. If desired, frost with Honey Glaze.

Honey Glaze: In small mixing bowl, combine confectioners' sugar, pecans and honey. Blend in milk until of spreading consistency.

*For use with Pillsbury's Best Self-Rising Flour, omit salt.

Twin loaves of moist, brown bread, ready in 3½ hours. It tastes like whole wheat bread, yet you don't need rye or whole wheat flour.

Caraway Bran Bread

  5½ to 6 cups Pillsbury's Best All Purpose
     Flour*
  I cup whole bran cereal
  2 tablespoons sugar
  2 teaspoons salt
  I teaspoon caraway seed, if desired
  I package active dry yeast
  I cup milk
  ¼ cup shortening
  ¼ cup dark molasses
  1½ cups warm water

OVEN 375°   2 LOAVES

In large mixer bowl, combine 2 cups of flour, bran cereal, sugar, salt, caraway seed and dry yeast. In saucepan, heat milk, shortening and molasses until milk is warm. (Shortening does not need to melt.) Add warm milk and water to flour mixture. Blend at lowest speed until moistened; beat 2 minutes at medium speed. By hand, stir in remaining flour to form a stiff dough. Cover; let rise in warm place until light and doubled in size, about I hour.

Punch down dough. Toss on well-floured surface until no longer sticky. Divide dough in half; shape into loaves. Place in well-greased 9x5-inch loaf pans. Cover; let rise in warm place until light and doubled in size, 45 to 60 minutes. Bake at 375° for 40 to 45 minutes until golden brown. Remove from pans; cool.

*For use with Pillsbury's Best Self-Rising Flour, omit salt.

How to make the fanciest peanut butter sandwiches in the block! Or, make some rolls plus a loaf for sandwiches or toast—it's ready in 3 hours.

Peanut Butter Bread 'N Rolls

  4½ to 5 cups Pillsbury's Best All Purpose
     Flour*
  ½ cup firmly packed brown sugar
  2 teaspoons salt
  2 packages active dry yeast
  2 cups milk
  ½ cup peanut butter
  2 tablespoons butter or margarine

OVEN 350°   2 LOAVES

In large mixer bowl, combine 2 cups of flour, brown sugar, salt and dry yeast. In saucepan, heat milk, peanut butter and butter until milk is warm. (Butter does not need to melt.) Add to flour mixture. Blend at lowest speed until moistened; beat 3 minutes at medium speed. By hand, stir in remaining flour to form a stiff dough. Knead on well-floured surface until smooth and no longer sticky, about I minute. Place in greased bowl, turning to grease top. Cover; let rise in warm place until light and doubled in size, about I hour.

Punch down dough; divide in half, shape into two loaves. Place in greased 9x5-inch loaf pans. Cover; let rise in warm place until light and doubled in size, about 45 minutes. Bake at 350° for 40 to 45 minutes until deep golden brown. Remove from pans; cool.

Tips: If desired, shape into 24 peanut butter rolls or I loaf and I2 rolls. Let rise; bake at 375° for I5 to 20 minutes until deep golden brown.

Spread slices of bread with jelly for delicious peanut butter and jelly sandwiches, or toast slices and spread with jam or honey for a special breakfast treat.

*For use with Pillsbury's Best Self-Rising Flour, omit salt.

MENU
After School Treat
Toasted Peanut Butter Bread
Jam or Honey
Fresh Fruit
Milk

A light bread with a nippy blend of garlic and cheese, easy made in 3 hours. Pop slices in toaster and bring on the spaghetti!

Garlic Cheese Toast

2¼ to 2½ cups Pillsbury's Best All Purpose Flour*
1 tablespoon sugar
1½ teaspoons salt
1 to 2 teaspoons (2 cloves) finely chopped garlic
1 package active dry yeast
1 cup milk
1 cup (4 oz.) shredded Cheddar cheese

OVEN 375°   1 LOAF

In large mixing bowl, combine 1 cup of flour, sugar, salt, garlic and dry yeast. In saucepan, heat milk and cheese until milk is warm. Add to flour mixture. Beat until smooth. Gradually stir in remaining flour to form a stiff dough. Knead on floured surface until smooth, about 5 minutes. Place in greased bowl, turning to grease top. Cover; let rise in warm place until light and doubled in size, about 1 hour.

Punch down dough; shape into loaf. Place in greased 9x5-inch loaf pan. Cover; let rise in warm place until light and doubled in size, about 1 hour. Bake at 375° for 45 to 50 minutes, until golden brown. Remove from pan; cool.

Tips: For delicious garlic toast, try slicing and toasting.

¼ to ½ teaspoon garlic powder may be used for garlic.

*For use with Pillsbury's Best Self-Rising Flour, omit salt.

28

Save your coffee cans for this festive and colorful bread with candied fruit, raisins and chopped almonds. A large recipe; great for gifts, too. Four hours.

Can-Pan Fruit Bread

    7 to 8 cups Pillsbury's Best All Purpose
       Flour*
  ½ cup sugar
    3 teaspoons salt
    3 packages active dry yeast
    2 cups milk
  ½ cup shortening
    2 eggs
    2 teaspoons vanilla
 1½ cups chopped mixed candied fruit
  ½ cup raisins
  ½ cup chopped blanched almonds

OVEN 350°   2 LARGE OR 6 SMALL LOAVES

In large mixer bowl, combine 3 cups of flour, sugar, salt and dry yeast. In saucepan, heat milk and shortening until milk is warm. (Shortening does not need to melt.) Add eggs, vanilla and warm milk to flour mixture. Blend at low speed until moistened; beat 3 minutes at medium speed. Stir in fruit, raisins and nuts. By hand, stir in remaining flour to form a stiff dough. Knead on floured surface until smooth and elastic, about 3 minutes. Place in greased bowl, turning to grease top. Cover; let rise in warm place until light and doubled in size, 1 to 1½ hours.

Punch down dough; divide in half. Shape into round loaves and place in two well-greased 8 or 9-inch layer pans, or divide into six parts and place in six well-greased 1-pound coffee cans. Cover; let rise in warm place until light and doubled in size, about 1 hour. Bake at 350° for 45 to 50 minutes for large loaves and 35 to 40 minutes for small loaves until golden brown. Remove from pans immediately. Cool and frost tops with Vanilla Frosting, page 12.

*For use with Pillsbury's Best Self-Rising Flour, omit salt.

29

Three hours to make a magnifique crusty bread in golden-brown braids. If you like compliments, go French for dinner tonight, madame!

French Bread Braids

5½ to 6 cups Pillsbury's Best All Purpose
   Flour*
3 teaspoons salt
1 tablespoon sugar
2 packages active dry yeast
2 tablespoons shortening
2 cups warm water
1 egg white, slightly beaten
1 tablespoon water

OVEN 375°   2 BRAIDS

In large mixer bowl, combine 3 cups of flour, salt, sugar and dry yeast. Add shortening and warm water. Blend at lowest speed until moistened; beat 3 minutes at medium speed. By hand, stir in remaining flour to form a stiff dough. Turn out on well-floured surface. Knead until smooth, about 3 minutes. Place in greased bowl, turning to grease top. Cover; let rise in warm place until light and doubled in size, about 1 hour.

Punch down dough; divide in half. Divide each half into three parts. Form each part into a strip 14 inches long. Braid the three together, sealing ends. Place on greased cookie sheet. Repeat with other half. Brush with mixture of egg white and water. Cover loosely and let rise until light and doubled in size, about 45 minutes. Brush again with egg white mixture. Bake at 375° for 35 to 40 minutes until golden brown.

Tip: For crusty rolls, shape dough into 24 rolls. Place on greased cookie sheets. Make slashes across top. Brush with egg white. Let rise. Bake at 375° for 20 to 25 minutes until golden brown.

*Pillsbury's Best Self-Rising Flour is not recommended for use in this recipe.

50 million Frenchmen can't be wrong about this bread. It's a poppy-seed loaf ready in about 3 hours to make your family say . . . Vive!

Crusty French Bread

5 to 5½ cups Pillsbury's Best All Purpose
   Flour*
1 tablespoon sugar
3 teaspoons salt
1 package active dry yeast
2 cups warm water
1 tablespoon shortening
1 egg white, slightly beaten
1 tablespoon water
Poppy seeds or sesame seeds, if desired

OVEN 375°   1 LARGE LOAF

In large mixing bowl, combine 2 cups of flour, sugar, salt and dry yeast. Add warm water and shortening. Beat until smooth. Stir in remaining flour to form a stiff dough. Knead on floured surface until no longer sticky, about 5 minutes. Place in greased bowl, turning to grease top. Cover; let rise in warm place until light and doubled in size, 1 to 1½ hours.

Punch down dough. Shape into one large long loaf, or two smaller long loaves; place on greased cookie sheet. Cover; let rise in warm place until light and doubled in size, about 45 minutes. Combine egg white and water. Brush over top of dough; sprinkle with poppy or sesame seeds. With very sharp knife, make 3 or 4 diagonal slashes ½ inch deep across top. Bake at 375° for 40 to 45 minutes until light golden brown.

Tip: For a crustier loaf, bake bread with a shallow pan of water on lower oven rack.

*Pillsbury's Best Self-Rising Flour is not recommended for use in this recipe.

30

Twin loaves of French-style bread, crusty and rich with sour cream. Give yourself 3 hours and you'll have warm crusty French bread.

Golden-Crust Bread

5½ to 6 cups Pillsbury's Best All Purpose
    Flour*
2 tablespoons sugar
3 teaspoons salt
1 package active dry yeast
1¼ cups warm water
1 cup dairy sour cream
2 tablespoons butter or margarine, melted
1 egg white, slightly beaten
1 tablespoon water

OVEN 375°   2 LOAVES

In large mixing bowl, combine 2 cups of flour, sugar, salt and dry yeast. Add warm water, sour cream and melted butter. Blend until smooth. Gradually stir in remaining flour to form a stiff dough. Knead on floured surface until dough is smooth and satiny, 5 to 7 minutes. Place in greased bowl, turning to grease top. Cover; let rise in warm place until light and doubled in size, 1 to 1½ hours.

Divide dough into two portions. On a floured surface, roll each portion to a 12x5-inch rectangle. Starting with 12-inch side, roll up jelly-roll fashion, sealing well after each turn. Pinch edges together to seal; pull to taper ends. Place seam-side down on greased cookie sheets. Cover; let rise in warm place until light and doubled in size, about 1 hour. Brush with mixture of egg white and water. With very sharp knife, gently make 3 or 4 diagonal slashes ½ inch deep across top. Bake at 375° for 40 to 45 minutes until golden brown.

*For use with Pillsbury's Best Self-Rising Flour, omit salt.

MENU
"Left-Over" Supper
Chicken and Vegetable Casserole
Lettuce Wedge with French Dressing
French Bread Braid
Raspberry Sherbet
Cookies
Beverage

Marbled loaves of white and whole wheat, warm from the oven in 3 hours. Make them braided or spiral.

Two-Tone Loaves

4 cups Pillsbury's Best All Purpose Flour*
¼ cup sugar
3 teaspoons salt
2 packages active dry yeast
2½ cups milk
¼ cup butter or margarine
¼ cup molasses
1½ to 2 cups whole wheat flour
1½ to 2 cups Pillsbury's Best All Purpose
    Flour*

OVEN 350°   2 LOAVES

In large mixer bowl, combine 4 cups of flour, sugar, salt and dry yeast. In saucepan, heat milk and butter until milk is warm. (Butter does not need to melt.) Add to flour mixture. Blend at lowest speed until moistened; beat 3 minutes at medium speed. Cover; let rise in warm place until light and doubled in size, about 45 minutes. Stir down; place half in another large bowl. By hand, add molasses and whole wheat flour to half of yeast mixture to form a stiff dough. Knead on well-floured surface until smooth and no longer sticky, about 3 minutes. Set aside. By hand, add 1½ to 2 cups of flour to remaining yeast mixture to form a stiff dough. Knead on well-floured surface until smooth and no longer sticky. Divide each dough in half. Roll out each to a 12x6-inch rectangle. Place 1 dark rectangle on 1 light rectangle. Roll up tightly, starting with 6-inch side. Seal edges and ends. Place seam-side down in well-greased 9x5-inch loaf pan. Repeat with other two rectangles. Cover; let rise in warm place until light and doubled in size, about 1 hour. Bake at 350° for 45 to 50 minutes until golden brown. Remove from pans; cool.

Tip: For a braided loaf, shape the two colors of dough into strips 10 inches long. Place 1 dark and 1 light together; coil around each other lightly. Fit into loaf pan. Bake as directed above.

*For use with Pillsbury's Best Self-Rising Flour, omit salt.

A shapely braid baked on a cookie sheet, that makes pretty golden slices, crowned with seeds. Plan three and a half hours in all.

County Fair Egg Bread

> 5 to 5½ cups Pillsbury's Best All Purpose
>   Flour*
> ¼ cup sugar
> 2 teaspoons salt
> I package active dry yeast
> 1½ cups milk
> ¼ cup shortening
> 2 eggs
> I egg white, slightly beaten
> I tablespoon water
>   Poppy seeds or sesame seeds

OVEN 375°   2 BRAIDED LOAVES

In large mixer bowl, combine 2 cups of flour, sugar, salt and dry yeast. In saucepan, heat milk and shortening until milk is warm. (Shortening does not need to melt.) Add eggs and warm milk to flour mixture. Blend at lowest speed until moistened; beat 3 minutes at medium speed. By hand, stir in remaining flour to form a stiff dough. Knead on floured surface until smooth and elastic, about 3 minutes. Place in greased bowl, turning to grease top. Cover; let rise in warm place until light and doubled in size, I to 1½ hours.

Punch down dough; divide into 6 portions. Shape each portion into a strip eight inches long by rolling between hands. Braid three strips together. Place braid on greased cookie sheet. Braid remaining three strips and place on cookie sheet. Cover; let rise in warm place until light and doubled in size, about 45 minutes. Brush with mixture of egg white and water. Sprinkle with poppy seeds or sesame seeds. Bake at 375° for 35 to 40 minutes until golden brown.

Tip: If desired, bake in two greased 9x5-inch loaf pans as directed above.

*For use with Pillsbury's Best Self-Rising Flour, omit salt.

A light and tender French bread, that smacks of onion. It can also be fashioned into savory hamburger buns. Ready in three hours' time.

French Onion Bread

> 5½ to 6 cups Pillsbury's Best All Purpose
>   Flour*
> 4 tablespoons (½ envelope) dry onion soup
>   mix
> 3 tablespoons sugar
> 2 teaspoons salt
> 2 packages active dry yeast
> 2 tablespoons shortening
> 2 cups warm water
> I egg white, slightly beaten
> I tablespoon water

OVEN 375°   2 LOAVES

In large mixer bowl, combine 2 cups of flour, onion soup mix, sugar, salt and dry yeast. Add shortening and warm water. Blend at lowest speed until moistened; beat 3 minutes at medium speed. By hand, stir in remaining flour to form a stiff dough. Knead on floured surface until smooth and elastic, about 3 minutes. Place in greased bowl, turning to grease top. Cover; let rise in warm place until light and doubled in size, I to 1½ hours.

Punch down dough; divide into two portions. On a floured surface, roll each portion to a 12x5-inch rectangle. Starting with 12-inch side, roll up jelly-roll fashion, sealing dough with heel of hands after each roll. Pinch edges together to seal and pull to taper ends. Place seam-side down, on greased cookie sheets. Cover; let rise in warm place until light and doubled in size, about I hour. Brush with mixture of egg white and water. With very sharp knife, gently make 3 or 4 diagonal slashes ½ inch deep across top. Bake at 375° for 35 to 40 minutes until golden brown.

Tip: If desired, dough may be shaped into 18 to 24 hamburger buns. Let rise about 30 minutes after shaping; bake at 375° for 15 to 18 minutes.

*For use with Pillsbury's Best Self-Rising Flour, omit salt.

Sure to be a favorite whether eaten as a sand-wich or served at a barbecue. Tastes like hours of work—but ready in less than three!

Butterflake Herb Loaf

  4½ to 5½ cups Pillsbury's Best All Purpose
      Flour*
  ¼ cup sugar
  3 teaspoons salt
  I package active dry yeast
1¼ cups milk
  ⅓ cup shortening
  2 eggs

Herb Butter

  ½ cup butter or margarine, softened
  ½ teaspoon caraway seed
  ½ teaspoon sweet basil
  ½ teaspoon grated onion
  ¼ teaspoon leaf oregano
  ⅛ teaspoon cayenne pepper
  I clove garlic, minced or ¼ teaspoon garlic
      powder

OVEN 350°   2 LOAVES

In large mixer bowl, combine 2 cups of flour, sugar, salt and dry yeast. In saucepan, heat milk and shortening until milk is warm. (Shortening does not need to melt.) Add eggs and warm milk to flour mixture. Blend at low-est speed until moistened; beat 3 minutes at medium speed. By hand, stir in remaining flour to form a stiff dough. Knead on floured surface until smooth and elastic, about 3 minutes. Place in greased bowl, turning to grease top. Cover; let rise in warm place until light and doubled in size, I to 1½ hours.

Punch down dough. Divide dough in half. Roll out one portion of dough on lightly floured surface to a 15x9-inch rectangle. Spread on half of the Herb Butter. Roll up towards you from 9-inch edge, as for shaping a loaf, page 22. Seal ends; place, seam-side down, in greased 9x5-inch loaf pan. Repeat with re-maining dough. Cover; let rise in warm place until dough reaches top of pan and corners are filled, I to 1½ hours. Bake at 350° for 30 to 35 minutes until golden brown.

Herb Butter: In small mixing bowl, combine all ingredients and mix until well blended.

*For use with Pillsbury's Best Self-Rising Flour, omit salt.

Rich with herbs and butter—basil, caraway and thyme combine to give these loaves the gour-met touch. Great for your next patio party! Give yourself about 3½ hours.

Herb and Butter Bread

  7½ to 8 cups Pillsbury's Best All Purpose
      Flour*
  ⅓ cup firmly packed brown sugar
  3 teaspoons salt
  I teaspoon sweet basil
  I teaspoon caraway seed
  ½ teaspoon thyme
  2 packages active dry yeast
2½ cups milk
  ½ cup butter or margarine

OVEN 375°   2 LOAVES

In large mixer bowl, combine 3 cups of flour, brown sugar, salt, basil, caraway seed, thyme and dry yeast. In saucepan, heat milk and but-ter until milk is warm. (Butter does not need to melt.) Add warm milk to flour mixture. Blend at lowest speed until moistened; beat 3 minutes at medium speed. By hand, stir in remaining flour to form a stiff dough. Knead on floured surface until smooth and elastic, about 5 minutes. Place in greased bowl, turn-ing to grease top. Cover; let rise in warm place until light and doubled in size, I to 1½ hours.

Punch down dough; divide into 2 parts. Shape each into a loaf, see page 22; place in greased 9x5-inch loaf pans. Cover; let rise in warm place until light and doubled in size, 45 to 60 minutes. Bake at 375° for 35 to 40 minutes until golden brown. Remove from pans imme-diately; cool.

*For use with Pillsbury's Best Self-Rising Flour, omit salt.

Rich and regal flavor in a moist, rye loaf, complete with raisins and a hint of orange. Give yourself 3 hours to make and bake.

Dark Orange Raisin Bread

  2 cups rye flour
  3 teaspoons salt
  2 tablespoons grated orange peel
  2 packages active dry yeast
  ½ cup molasses
  ¼ cup shortening
  2 cups warm water
  I cup raisins
  4 to 4½ cups Pillsbury's Best All Purpose
    Flour*

OVEN 350°   2 LOAVES

In large mixer bowl, combine rye flour, salt, orange peel and dry yeast. Add molasses, shortening and warm water. Blend at lowest speed until moistened; beat 3 minutes at medium speed. By hand, stir in raisins and flour to form a stiff dough. Knead on well-floured surface until smooth, about 3 minutes. Place in greased bowl, turning to grease top. Cover; let rise in warm place until light and doubled in size, about I hour.

Divide dough in half; shape into 2 loaves. Place loaves in greased 9x5-inch loaf pans or on greased cookie sheets. Cover; let rise in warm place until light and doubled in size, about 45 minutes. Bake at 350° for 45 to 50 minutes until golden brown. Cool.

*For use with Pillsbury's Best Self-Rising Flour, omit salt.

MENU
Family Breakfast
Orange Juice
Scrambled Eggs
Bacon
Toasted Dark Orange Raisin Bread
Beverage

A great way to get a rye-tasting bread with no rye flour, but a combination of prunes, whole bran cereal and molasses. A moist, heavy bread in five and a half hours . . . best next day.

Prune Bran Loaf

  I½ cups hot water
  I½ cups whole bran cereal
    I cup cut-up cooked prunes
  ½ cup molasses
  ⅓ cup shortening
  5½ to 6 cups Pillsbury's Best All Purpose
    Flour*
  3 teaspoons salt
  2 packages active dry yeast
  2 eggs
  I tablespoon butter or margarine, melted

OVEN 350°   2 LOAVES

In saucepan, bring water to boil; add whole bran cereal, prunes, molasses and shortening. Remove from heat and cool to lukewarm. In large mixer bowl, combine 3 cups of flour, salt and dry yeast. Add warm liquid and eggs to dry ingredients. Blend at low speed until dry ingredients are moistened; beat 3 minutes at medium speed. By hand, stir in remaining flour to form a stiff dough. Cover; let rise in warm place until doubled in size, 2 to 2½ hours.

Divide dough in half. Roll out each portion on floured surface to a I4x7-inch rectangle. Roll up starting with 7-inch side. Place seam-side down in well-greased 9x5-inch loaf pans. Cover; let rise in warm place until light and doubled in size, I to I½ hours. Bake at 350° for 40 to 45 minutes until golden brown. Brush tops with melted butter.

*For use with Pillsbury's Best Self-Rising Flour, omit salt.

Corn muffin mix and mushroom soup combine in this interesting buffet bread. Break apart loaves, golden and light from only an hour's work. Note the tip to create a cheesy bread with cheese soup.

Muffin Mix Buffet Bread

   4 to 4½ cups Pillsbury's Best All Purpose
      Flour*
   1 package Pillsbury Golden Corn Muffin
      Mix (reserve 2 tablespoons)
   ½ teaspoon salt
   2 packages active dry yeast
   ¾ cup warm water
   1 can (10½ oz.) condensed cream of
      mushroom soup
   ¼ cup butter or margarine, softened
   ⅓ cup butter or margarine, melted

OVEN 375°   2 LOAVES

In large mixer bowl, combine 1 cup of flour with remaining ingredients except melted butter. Blend at lowest speed until dry ingredients are moistened; beat 3 minutes at medium speed. By hand, stir in remaining flour to form a stiff dough. Knead on floured surface until smooth and satiny, about 3 minutes. Divide dough in half. Roll out each portion on floured surface to a 9x5-inch rectangle. Cut each portion crosswise into nine strips, 1 inch wide. Place in well-greased 9x5-inch loaf pans. Pour melted butter over each loaf and sprinkle with reserved muffin mix. Let rise in warm place until light, about 30 minutes. Bake at 375° for 20 to 25 minutes until golden brown. Remove from pans immediately.

Tips: If desired, use 1 can (10¾ oz.) condensed Cheddar cheese soup for mushroom soup.

Make two 10x6-inch loaves by rolling out dough to two 10x6-inch rectangles and slice into ten 1-inch slices. Place in two well-greased 10x6-inch pans.

*Not recommended for use with Pillsbury's Best Self-Rising Flour.

A hearty, English-style bran bread sparked with dried beef and chives. Great with luncheon salads. Allow 3 hours plus time to cool.

Country Garden Casserole Bread

   3¼ to 3¾ cups Pillsbury's Best All Purpose
      Flour*
   1 cup (3 oz.) minced dried beef
   ½ cup whole bran cereal
   ¼ cup chopped chives
   2 tablespoons sugar
   1 teaspoon salt
   1 package active dry yeast
   1¼ cups milk
   ¼ cup shortening
   1 egg

OVEN 375°   1 ROUND LOAF

In large mixer bowl, combine 2 cups of flour, dried beef, bran cereal, chives, sugar, salt and dry yeast. In saucepan, heat milk and shortening until milk is warm. (Shortening does not need to melt.) Add egg and warm milk to flour mixture. Blend at lowest speed until moistened; beat 2 minutes at medium speed. By hand, stir in remaining flour to form a stiff dough. Knead on floured surface until smooth, about 3 minutes. Place in greased bowl, turning to grease top. Cover; let rise in warm place until light and doubled in size, about 1 hour.

Punch down dough; shape into a smooth, round loaf. Place in greased 1½-quart baking dish. Cover; let rise in warm place until light and doubled in size, about 1 hour. Bake at 375° for 40 to 45 minutes until golden brown. Remove from baking dish. Brush with melted butter; cool.

*For use with Pillsbury's Best Self-Rising Flour, omit salt.

Chunks o' cheese trapped in round molasses and cornmeal loaves. What an attractive bread with golden chunks peaking through each slice! Ready to serve in about 3 hours.

Chunk O' Cheese Bread

  2 cups water
½ cup cornmeal
  2 teaspoons salt
½ cup molasses
  2 tablespoons butter or margarine
  5 to 6 cups Pillsbury's Best All Purpose
      Flour*
  1 package active dry yeast
½ pound (8 oz.) American cheese

OVEN 350°   2 LOAVES

In medium saucepan, combine water, cornmeal and salt. Bring to boil over medium-high heat, stirring constantly; cook until slightly thickened. Remove from heat. Add molasses and butter. Cool to lukewarm. In large mixing bowl, combine 2 cups of flour and dry yeast. Add cornmeal mixture. Blend well. Stir in remaining flour to form a stiff dough. Knead on well-floured surface until smooth and elastic, about 5 minutes. (Dough will be somewhat sticky.) Place in greased bowl, turning to grease top. Cover; let rise in warm place until light and doubled in size, about 1 hour.

Cut cheese into ½-inch cubes. Punch down dough. Work cheese into dough, one-fourth at a time, until cubes are evenly distributed. Divide into two parts. Shape into two round loaves, covering cheese cubes. Place in two 8 or 9-inch round layer pans, well-greased and sprinkled with cornmeal. Cover; let rise in warm place until light and doubled in size, about 1 hour. Bake at 350° for 55 to 60 minutes until deep golden brown.

Tip: If desired, bake loaves in two 1½-quart casseroles, well-greased and sprinkled with cornmeal.

*For use with Pillsbury's Best Self-Rising Flour, omit salt.

Dill and Cheddar cheese take a merry whirl in a rye or whole wheat loaf that has overtones of onion. It can be the star of your supper in less than four hours.

Cheese Roll Loaf

  2 cups rye or whole wheat flour
⅓ cup sugar
  3 teaspoons salt
  2 packages active dry yeast
  1 can (10½ oz.) condensed onion soup
  1 cup water
¼ cup shortening
3½ to 4 cups Pillsbury's Best All Purpose
      Flour*
  4 tablespoons butter or margarine, melted
  1 teaspoon dill seed
  2 cups shredded Cheddar cheese
      Milk
      Sesame seeds

OVEN 350°   2 LOAVES

In large mixer bowl, combine rye flour, sugar, salt and dry yeast. In saucepan, heat soup, water and shortening until warm. (Shortening does not need to melt.) Add warm liquid to flour mixture. Blend at low speed until moistened; beat 3 minutes at medium speed. By hand, stir in all purpose flour to form a stiff dough. Knead on floured surface until smooth and elastic, about 3 minutes. Place in greased bowl, turning to grease top. Cover; let rise in warm place until light and doubled in size, 1 to 1½ hours.

Punch down dough; divide in half. Roll out each portion of dough on floured surface to a 12x9-inch rectangle. Brush each with 2 tablespoons melted butter; sprinkle with dill seed and cheese. Starting with 9-inch side, roll up; seal edges. Place seam-side down in well-greased 9x5-inch loaf pans. Cover; let rise in warm place until light and doubled in size, about 1 hour. Brush with milk; sprinkle on sesame seeds. Bake at 350° for 50 to 60 minutes until golden brown. Remove from pans immediately. Cool.

*For use with Pillsbury's Best Self-Rising Flour, omit salt.

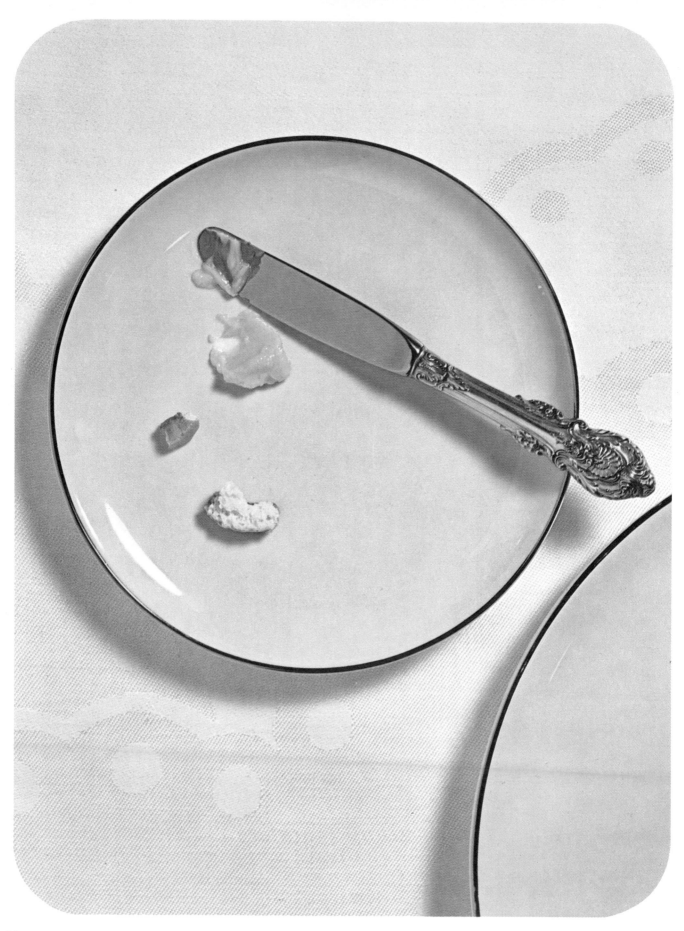

Dinner & Luncheon Rolls

● Rolls are the charming accessories that enhance your dinner or luncheon and show your thoughtfulness and flair. In this collection of Bake Off entries, you will find everything from the exotic to the familiar, from airy lovelies fit for a queen, to hearty barbecue buns, and some new ideas for shapes, too. Many use the no-knead method to save you work, and all of them will gather you compliments whenever you serve them.

Shaping Rolls

● Rolls can feature many shapes. Pick a shape or combine two or three. Then, follow the easy directions with each photo for a pretty basket of homemade rolls.

Pan Rolls

Shape dough into balls about 1½ inches in diameter. Place in greased 8-inch round or square pan so that sides just touch. For rolls that break apart more easily, brush with butter.

Finger Rolls

Divide dough into pieces about the size of walnuts. Shape each piece into a roll about 4 inches long. Place in greased 8-inch square pan; sides should just touch to make two rows in pan.

Crescents

Roll out dough to a circle about ¼-inch thick. (For larger amounts of dough, you may wish to divide dough in half and roll out two circles.) Cut circle into wedges 2½ to 3 inches across wide end. Starting with wide end, roll up each wedge toward point. Place point-side down on greased cookie sheets. Curve ends to form crescent.

Fan-Tans

Roll out dough on well-floured surface to a 15x9-inch rectangle, about ¼-inch thick. Cut into 9x1½-inch strips. Stack 5 strips together; cut into 1½-inch pieces. Place each stack, cut-side up, in greased muffin cup.

Cloverleaf Rolls

Shape dough into small balls about 1 inch in diameter. Place three balls in each greased muffin cup.

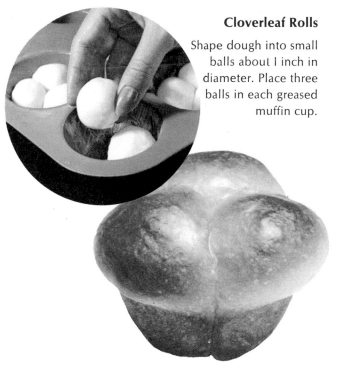

Quick Cloverleaf Rolls

Shape dough into balls about 2 inches in diameter. Place in greased muffin cups. With kitchen scissors, cut balls in half almost to bottom; then in quarters.

Bow Knots

Divide dough into pieces the size of walnuts. With buttered hands, shape each into a strip about 9 inches long by rolling between hands. Tie in loose knots, being careful not to stretch dough. Place on greased cookie sheets.

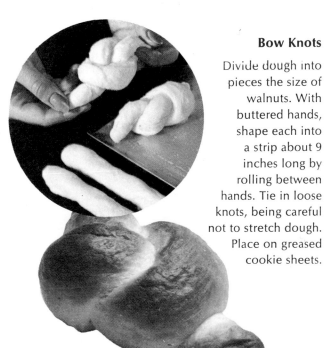

Quick Parkerhouse Rolls

Divide dough into pieces the size of walnuts. Flatten each with palm of hand into an oval shape. Brush with melted butter. With knife, crease each lengthwise slightly off center. Fold ovals over to make half circles; press edges to seal. Place on greased cookie sheets.

Egg custard mix gives these dinner rolls a special richness in flavor and color. Only an hour and a half and you can serve them hot from the oven.

Parkerhouse Easy's

  3½ to 4 cups Pillsbury's Best All Purpose
    Flour*
  I teaspoon salt
  2 packages active dry yeast
  I package (3 oz.) egg custard mix
I¼ cups warm water
 ¼ cup butter or margarine, softened

OVEN 400°   16 to 24 ROLLS

In large mixer bowl, combine 2 cups of flour with remaining ingredients. Blend at low speed until moistened; beat 3 minutes at medium speed. By hand, stir in remaining flour to form a stiff dough. Knead on floured surface about 2 minutes. Roll out to a 20x8-inch rectangle. Cut in half lengthwise making two 20x4-inch strips. With knife handle, crease each strip lengthwise, slightly off center. Fold along crease. Gently pull and shape each strip to a 24-inch length. Cut each into twelve 2-inch or eight 3-inch slices. Place on greased cookie sheets. Cover; let rise in warm place until light, 45 to 60 minutes. Bake at 400° for 10 to 12 minutes until golden brown. Serve hot.

*For use with Pillsbury's Best Self-Rising Flour, omit salt.

Southern-style dinner rolls in any shape you fancy. Light and golden, warm from the oven in 2 hours.

Old Plantation Rolls

  3½ to 3¾ cups Pillsbury's Best All Purpose
    Flour*
  2 tablespoons sugar
  I teaspoon salt
 ½ teaspoon baking powder
 ¼ teaspoon soda
  I package active dry yeast
  I cup milk
 ¼ cup butter or margarine
  I egg

OVEN 375°   16 ROLLS

In large mixer bowl, combine 2 cups of flour, sugar, salt, baking powder, soda and dry yeast. In saucepan, heat milk and butter until milk

is warm. (Butter does not need to melt.) Add egg and warm milk to flour mixture. Blend at lowest speed until moistened; beat 3 minutes at medium speed. By hand, stir in remaining flour to form a stiff dough. Cover; let rise in warm place until light and doubled in size, about I hour.

Punch down dough; toss on floured surface until no longer sticky. Shape into 16 rolls as desired. Cover; let rise in warm place until light and doubled in size, about 30 minutes. Bake at 375° for 15 to 18 minutes until golden brown.

*For use with Pillsbury's Best Self-Rising Flour, omit salt, baking powder and soda.

There's just a hint of lemon in these delicate rolls, easy made in 2 hours without kneading. They'll be the talk of your dinner table!

Table Talk Rolls

  3 to 3¼ cups Pillsbury's Best All Purpose
    Flour*
  2 tablespoons sugar
  I teaspoon salt
  I teaspoon grated lemon peel
  I package active dry yeast
 ¾ cup milk
  2 tablespoons butter or margarine
  I egg

OVEN 375°   16 ROLLS

In small mixer bowl, combine I cup of flour, sugar, salt, lemon peel and dry yeast. In saucepan, heat milk and butter until milk is warm. (Butter does not need to melt.) Add egg and warm milk to flour mixture. Blend at lowest speed until moistened; beat 3 minutes at medium speed. By hand, stir in remaining flour to form a stiff dough. Cover; let rise in warm place until light and doubled in size, about 45 minutes.

Toss dough on well-floured surface until no longer sticky. Roll out to an 8-inch square. Cut into 16 squares. Coat each with flour. Place on greased cookie sheet. Cover; let rise in warm place until light and doubled in size, about 30 minutes. Bake at 375° for 15 to 18 minutes until light golden brown.

*For use with Pillsbury's Best Self-Rising Flour, omit salt.

MENU
Company Dinner
Roast Leg of Lamb
Scalloped Potatoes
Buttered Peas and Onions
Mint-Lime Gelatin Salad
Crusty Dinner Rolls
Ice Cream Parfait Pie
Beverage

Big, beautiful and crusty, these handsome yeast rolls have the open-grained heartiness of French bread. Make them up in about three hours.

Crusty Dinner Rolls

> 6 to 6½ cups Pillsbury's Best All Purpose Flour*
> 2 tablespoons sugar
> 3 teaspoons salt
> 2 packages active dry yeast
> ¼ cup shortening
> 2 egg whites
> 2 cups warm water
> ¼ cup cornmeal
> 2 egg yolks
> 1 tablespoon water
> Poppy seeds or sesame seeds

OVEN 400°   24 ROLLS

In large mixing bowl, combine 3 cups of flour, sugar, salt and dry yeast. Add shortening, egg whites and warm water and mix until well blended. By hand, stir in remaining flour to form a stiff dough. Knead on floured surface until smooth and elastic, 3 to 5 minutes. Place in greased bowl, turning to grease top. Cover; let rise in warm place until light and doubled in size, 1 to 1½ hours.

Punch down dough. With floured fingers, shape into round or oval rolls. Dip bottoms in cornmeal; place on greased cookie sheets. Cover; let rise in warm place until light and doubled in size, about 1 hour. With sharp knife, make one large slash across top of roll. Combine egg yolks with water. Brush carefully on rolls. Sprinkle on poppy seeds or sesame seeds, if desired. Bake at 400° for 20 to 25 minutes until golden brown.

Tip: For extra crusty rolls, place a shallow pan of hot water on bottom rack of oven.

*For use with Pillsbury's Best Self-Rising Flour, omit salt.

Rich and flaky coiled dinner rolls that bake up light and buttery. Start about 3 hours before dinner time.

Butter-Flake Rolls

> 4 to 5 cups Pillsbury's Best All Purpose Flour*
> 1 tablespoon sugar
> 2 packages active dry yeast
> ¾ cup warm water
> ½ cup butter or margarine, softened
> ¼ cup sugar
> 1 teaspoon salt
> 3 eggs
> Melted butter

OVEN 375°   24 ROLLS

In mixing bowl, combine 1 cup of flour, 1 tablespoon sugar, dry yeast and warm water; mix well. Cover; let rise in warm place until light and bubbly, 20 to 30 minutes. In large mixer bowl, combine butter, sugar, salt and eggs; beat until well blended. Add the yeast mixture; mix well. By hand, gradually add 3 to 4 cups flour to form a stiff dough. Knead on floured surface about 30 strokes. Place in greased bowl, turning to grease top. Cover; let rise in warm place until light and doubled in size, 1 to 1½ hours.

Punch down dough; divide in half. Roll out each half on floured surface to a 12x8-inch rectangle. Cut into 1-inch strips. Roll each strip in melted butter. Coil each strip to form a "snail" in greased muffin cups. Cover; let rise in warm place until doubled in size, about 30 minutes. Bake at 375° for 12 to 15 minutes until golden brown.

*For use with Pillsbury's Best Self-Rising Flour, omit salt.

Triple treat in 3 hours. A cloverleaf roll with one section white, one whole wheat and one cornmeal.

Three-Way Dinner Rolls

4¾ to 5 cups Pillsbury's Best All Purpose
    Flour*
⅓ cup sugar
 3 teaspoons salt
 I package active dry yeast
 2 cups warm water
⅓ cup shortening
 2 eggs
½ cup cornmeal
 I cup whole wheat flour

OVEN 400°   24 ROLLS

In large mixing bowl, combine 3 cups of flour, sugar, salt and dry yeast. Add warm water, shortening and eggs; beat until smooth. Divide batter into 3 parts by placing in 3 medium mixing bowls. To the first part, stir in cornmeal and ½ to ⅔ cup flour to form a stiff dough; to second, stir in whole wheat flour to form a stiff dough; to third, stir in I to I¼ cups flour to form a stiff dough. Cover each; let rise in warm place until light and doubled in size, about I hour.

Toss each dough on floured surface until no longer sticky. Shape into cloverleaf rolls, placing one ball of each dough in greased muffin cups. Cover; let rise in warm place until light and doubled in size, about I hour. Bake at 400° for I5 to 20 minutes until golden brown.

*For use with Pillsbury's Best Self-Rising Flour, omit salt.

Potato soup and chives go into these self-buttered potato dinner rolls, sprinkled with celery seed. Serve in less than two hours.

Vichyssoise Feather Fans

4¾ to 5¼ cups Pillsbury's Best All Purpose
    Flour*
 2 tablespoons sugar
 I tablespoon chopped chives
½ teaspoon salt
 2 packages active dry yeast
⅓ cup milk
½ cup butter or margarine
 I can (10½ oz.) condensed cream of
    potato soup
 2 eggs
 I tablespoon butter or margarine, melted
 I teaspoon celery seed, if desired

OVEN 400°   24 ROLLS

In large mixer bowl, combine 2 cups of flour, sugar, chives, salt and dry yeast. In saucepan, heat milk and butter until milk is warm. (Butter does not need to melt.) Blend in soup; add to flour mixture along with eggs. Blend at low speed until moistened; beat 3 minutes at medium speed. By hand, stir in remaining flour to form a stiff dough. Cover; let rise in warm place until doubled in size, 45 to 60 minutes.

Roll out on well-floured surface to an I8x12-inch rectangle. Brush with melted butter; sprinkle with celery seed. Cut I8-inch side into twelve I½-inch strips. Stack 3 strips together; then cut each into six 2-inch pieces. Place, cut-side up, in greased muffin cups, spreading tops apart slightly. Cover; let rise in warm place until light, about 30 minutes. Bake at 400° for I5 to I8 minutes until golden brown.

Tip: If desired, substitute I can (I0¼ oz.) frozen cream of potato soup, thawed, for the condensed soup.

*For use with Pillsbury's Best Self-Rising Flour, omit salt.

A delightful buttermilk flavor with the ease of no-knead dough . . . serve tender, warm dinner rolls in 2½ hours.

Buttercrust Flake-Aparts

4¼ to 5 cups Pillsbury's Best All Purpose
    Flour*
⅓ cup sugar
2 teaspoons salt
½ teaspoon soda
2 packages active dry yeast
1½ cups buttermilk or sour milk
½ cup butter
    Melted butter

OVEN 400°   20 ROLLS

In large mixer bowl, combine 2 cups of flour, sugar, salt, soda and dry yeast. In saucepan, heat buttermilk and butter until buttermilk is warm. (Butter does not need to melt.) Add to flour mixture. Blend at lowest speed until moistened. Beat 2 minutes at medium speed. By hand, stir in remaining flour to form a stiff dough. Cover; let rise in warm place until light and doubled in size, about 1 hour.

Punch down dough. Roll out on floured surface to a 15-inch square. Brush with melted butter. Cut into strips 1½ inches wide; stack five strips together. Cut into pieces 1½ inches long. Place cut-side down in greased muffin cups. Cover; let rise until light and doubled in size, about 30 minutes. Bake at 400° for 15 to 20 minutes until golden brown. Serve warm.

*For use with Pillsbury's Best Self-Rising Flour, omit salt.

Parmesan and Cheddar cheese get together in these golden dinner rolls. Cloverleaf shaped from three tiny pinwheels in a muffin cup. About three hours.

Clover Cheese Rolls

    5 to 5½ cups Pillsbury's Best All Purpose
      Flour*
⅓ cup sugar
 2 teaspoons salt
 2 packages active dry yeast
1½ cups milk
 ½ cup shortening
  1 egg
 3 tablespoons butter or margarine, melted
 ¾ cup grated Parmesan cheese

Cheese Topping
   1 cup shredded Cheddar cheese
   2 tablespoons butter or margarine, melted
  ½ teaspoon onion salt or plain salt
  ⅛ teaspoon cayenne pepper

OVEN 400°   24 ROLLS

In large mixer bowl, combine 2 cups of flour, sugar, salt and dry yeast. In saucepan, heat milk and shortening until milk is warm. (Shortening does not need to melt.) Add egg and warm milk to flour mixture. Blend at lowest speed until moistened; beat 3 minutes at medium speed. By hand, stir in remaining flour to form a stiff dough. Knead on floured surface until smooth and elastic, about 3 minutes. Place in greased bowl, turning to grease top. Cover; let rise in warm place until light and doubled in size, 1 to 1½ hours.

Punch down dough; divide in thirds. Roll out one third of dough on floured surface to a 15x7-inch rectangle. Brush with 1 tablespoon melted butter; sprinkle on ¼ cup Parmesan cheese. Cut lengthwise into two 15x3½-inch strips. Roll up each strip, starting with 15-inch side; seal edges. Cut each into 12 slices. Place 3 slices, cut-side down, in well-greased muffin cups. Repeat with remaining dough. Cover; let rise in warm place until light and doubled in size, 30 to 45 minutes. Bake at 400° for 12 to 15 minutes until golden brown. Remove from oven; if desired, place a teaspoonful of Cheese Topping on each. Return to oven to melt cheese, 1 to 2 minutes.

Cheese Topping: In small mixing bowl, combine topping ingredients; mix well.

*For use with Pillsbury's Best Self-Rising Flour, omit salt.

A new flavor twist to crescent dinner rolls. Parmesan cheese is sprinkled over each before rolling up. Dough keeps well in refrigerator for easy rolls in about 1½ hours.

Parmesan Honor Rolls

 5 cups Pillsbury's Best All Purpose Flour*
¼ cup sugar
 1 teaspoon salt
 1 package active dry yeast
 1 cup butter or margarine
 1 cup milk
 2 eggs
   Melted butter
   Parmesan cheese

OVEN 375°   40 ROLLS

In large mixing bowl, combine flour, sugar, salt and dry yeast. Cut in butter until particles are coarse. In saucepan, heat milk until warm. Add eggs and warm milk to flour mixture. Mix until well blended. Cover; chill 2 to 3 hours. Divide dough into 5 portions. Roll out one part on floured surface to a 9-inch circle. Brush with melted butter; sprinkle with grated Parmesan cheese. Cut into 8 wedges. Roll wedge, starting with wide end and rolling to point. Place point-side down on greased cookie sheet. Repeat process with remaining portions. Let rise in warm place until light and doubled in size, about 1 hour. Bake at 375° for 15 to 18 minutes until golden brown.

Tips: On humid days, use 5½ cups flour.

Dough may be stored in refrigerator up to 3 days and baked as needed.

To make delicious plain crescent dinner rolls, just omit the Parmesan cheese.

For quick 'n easy Parmesan rolls, sprinkle Pillsbury Refrigerated Quick Crescent Dinner Rolls with Parmesan cheese before rolling up and baking as directed on package.

*For use with Pillsbury's Best Self-Rising Flour, use 5½ cups flour and omit salt.

Have yourself a whirl inventing crazy shapes for these potato bread dinner rolls. Shine them up with honey glaze in about 2½ hours.

Honey Crust Whirligigs

 3¾ to 4 cups Pillsbury's Best All Purpose
　　Flour*
　1 cup Pillsbury Hungry Jack Mashed
　　Potato Flakes
 ¼ cup sugar
 2 teaspoons salt
 1 package active dry yeast
 1¼ cups milk
 ⅓ cup shortening
 2 eggs
 3 tablespoons butter or margarine,
　　softened
 3 tablespoons honey

OVEN 400°　　　　　　　　　　20 ROLLS

In large mixer bowl, combine 1 cup of flour, potato flakes, sugar, salt and dry yeast. In saucepan, heat milk and shortening until milk is warm. (Shortening does not need to melt.) Add eggs and warm milk to flour mixture. Blend at lowest speed until moistened; beat 3 minutes at medium speed. By hand, stir in remaining flour to form a stiff dough. Knead on floured surface until smooth and elastic, about 3 minutes. Place in greased bowl, turning to grease top. Cover; let rise in warm place until light and doubled in size, 1 to 1½ hours. Punch down dough; divide into 20 pieces. Using buttered hands, shape each into a strip 10 inches long by rolling between hands. Wind each loosely around finger; drop into greased muffin cups at various angles. Combine butter and honey. Brush over tops of rolls. Cover; let rise in warm place until light and doubled in size, about 45 minutes. Bake at 400° for 12 to 15 minutes until golden brown. Remove from pans immediately.

Tip: Make delicious plain dinner rolls by omitting the butter-honey glaze.

*For use with Pillsbury's Best Self-Rising Flour, omit salt.

Rich egg rolls host a buttery, golden onion topping. Serve warm in three hours. Best made and served the same day. What a compliment to hamburgers!

Golden Onion Rolls

 2½ to 3 cups Pillsbury's Best All Purpose
　　Flour*
 2 tablespoons sugar
 ½ teaspoon salt
 1 package active dry yeast
 ¾ cup milk
 2 tablespoons shortening
 2 eggs (slightly beat and reserve 2
　　tablespoons)
　Poppy seeds

<u>Onion Topping</u>
 2 tablespoons instant minced onion,
　　reconstituted or 1 cup chopped onion
 2 tablespoons butter or margarine
 ⅛ teaspoon salt
 1 tablespoon reserved egg
 1 tablespoon milk

OVEN 375°　　　　　　　ABOUT 18 ROLLS

In large mixer bowl, combine 1 cup of flour, sugar, salt and dry yeast. In saucepan, heat milk and shortening until milk is warm. (Shortening does not need to melt.) Add warm milk and egg to flour mixture. Blend at low speed until moistened; beat 2 minutes at medium speed. By hand, stir in remaining flour. Knead on floured surface until smooth and elastic, about 3 minutes. Place in greased bowl, turning to grease top. Cover; let rise in warm place until light and doubled in size, 1 to 1½ hours. Prepare Onion Topping.

Shape dough into 2-inch balls; place on greased cookie sheets. Make a large indentation in center of each with finger. Spoon about 1 teaspoon of Onion Topping into center of each. Brush tops of rolls with 1 tablespoon of the reserved egg. Sprinkle with poppy seeds. Cover; let rise in warm place until doubled in size, about 45 minutes. Bake at 375° for 12 to 16 minutes until golden brown. Serve warm.

<u>Onion Topping</u>: Sauté onion in butter until golden. Stir in salt and mixture of 1 tablespoon of reserved egg and milk. Cool.

*For use with Pillsbury's Best Self-Rising Flour, increase flour to 3 to 3½ cups and omit salt.

The French have a word for buttery, tender, light rolls. They call it brioche and you can make it yours — quick 'n easy in 1½ hours.

Flaky Butter Brioche

5¼ to 5¾ cups Pillsbury's Best All Purpose
    Flour*
⅓ cup sugar
1 teaspoon salt
2 packages active dry yeast
1¼ cups milk
½ cup butter or margarine
2 eggs

OVEN 350°   24 ROLLS

In large mixer bowl, combine 3 cups of flour, sugar, salt and dry yeast. In saucepan, heat milk and butter until milk is warm. (Butter does not need to melt.) Add eggs and warm milk to flour mixture. Blend at lowest speed until moistened; beat at medium speed 3 minutes. By hand, stir in remaining flour to form a stiff dough. Knead on floured surface until smooth, 2 to 3 minutes.

Divide dough into 24 equal parts. Remove about ⅕ of dough from each part; shape all parts into smooth balls. Place large balls in greased brioche or medium muffin cups, making a deep indentation in center with finger. Place smaller balls in indentation. Cover; let rise in warm place until light and doubled in size, about 45 minutes. Brush tops with milk. Bake at 350° for 20 to 22 minutes until golden brown.

*For use with Pillsbury's Best Self-Rising Flour, omit salt.

You can count on these light and tender rolls for busy days. Make up dough and refrigerate; shape and bake when company comes.

Country Company Rolls

    4 to 4¼ cups Pillsbury's Best All Purpose
      Flour*
    ⅓ cup sugar
    2 teaspoons salt
    I package active dry yeast
    1¼ cups milk
    ½ cup shortening
    I egg

OVEN 400°   24 ROLLS

In large mixer bowl, combine 2 cups of flour, sugar, salt and dry yeast. In saucepan, heat milk and shortening until milk is warm. (Shortening does not need to melt.) Add egg and warm milk to flour mixture. Blend at lowest speed until moistened; beat 3 minutes at medium speed. By hand, stir in remaining flour to form a stiff dough. Cover. Store in refrigerator, up to 2 days, until ready to use. Shape dough into balls, about 2 inches in diameter. Place in greased muffin cups. Brush with melted butter. Cover; let rise in warm place until light and doubled in size, 2 to 2½ hours. Bake at 400° for 12 to 15 minutes until golden brown.

Tip: If desired, dough need not be refrigerated. Cover dough after mixing; let rise in warm place until light and doubled in size, about 1½ hours. Shape into rolls; let rise until light, 45 to 60 minutes. Bake at 400° for 12 to 15 minutes.

*For use with Pillsbury's Best Self-Rising Flour, omit salt.

Rosy-hued wrap-ups take their color from tomato juice, their spark from cheese and herbs. Tasty and ready in 2½ hours.

Hattie's Garden Crescents

    I package Pillsbury Hot Roll Mix
    ¼ cup warm water
    ½ cup warm tomato juice
    I tablespoon onion flakes
    I tablespoon celery flakes
    ½ teaspoon ground sage
    ½ teaspoon garlic salt
    I egg
      Parmesan cheese

OVEN 400°   16 ROLLS

Soften yeast included in hot roll mix package in water. In large mixing bowl, combine tomato juice, onion flakes, celery flakes, sage and garlic salt. Blend in egg and yeast. Add the flour mixture; blend well. Cover; let rise in warm place until light and doubled in size, 45 to 60 minutes. Divide dough into two parts. Roll each on lightly floured surface to a 12-inch circle. Sprinkle with cheese. Cut each circle into 8 wedges. Roll up, starting with wide end and rolling to point. Place point-side down on greased cookie sheets, curving ends to form crescent. Cover; let rise in warm place until light and doubled in size, 45 to 60 minutes. Bake at 400° for 12 to 15 minutes until golden brown.

Y'all will have seconds — or thirds — of these warm and golden Southern delights. Moist and crunchy in 1 hour and 45 minutes.

Southern Cornmeal Rolls

    I cup cornmeal
    1½ cups boiling water
    ½ cup milk
    ½ cup butter or margarine
    4¼ to 5 cups Pillsbury's Best All Purpose
      Flour*
    ¼ cup sugar
    2 teaspoons salt
    2 packages active dry yeast
    I egg

OVEN 400°   24 ROLLS

In large mixer bowl, combine cornmeal and boiling water until thoroughly mixed. Add milk and butter; stir until butter is softened. Add 2 cups of flour, sugar, salt, dry yeast and egg. Blend at lowest speed until moistened; beat 3 minutes at medium speed. By hand, stir in remaining flour to form a stiff dough. Knead on well-floured surface until smooth and no longer sticky, about 3 minutes. Place in greased bowl, turning to grease top. Cover; let rise in warm place until light and doubled in size, about 45 minutes.

Shape dough into 24 plain or cloverleaf rolls. Place in greased muffin cups. Cover; let rise in warm place until light and doubled in size, about 30 minutes. Bake at 400° for 15 to 18 minutes until golden brown.

*For use with Pillsbury's Best Self-Rising Flour, increase flour to 5 to 5½ cups and omit salt.

49

MENU

Patio Dinner Party

Standing Rib Roast of Beef
Baked Potatoes with Sour Cream
Melon Ball Salad
Smoky Barbecue Buns
Onion Rye Rolls
Herb Stickles, Porch Supper Braids
Lemon Chiffon Pie
Beverage

Smoky Barbecue Buns

3½ to 4 cups Pillsbury's Best All Purpose
    Flour*
  1 tablespoon sugar
  1 teaspoon salt
  1 package active dry yeast
1¼ cups warm water
  1 tablespoon butter or margarine, softened
  2 teaspoons barbecue seasoning
 ¼ teaspoon liquid smoke
  2 egg whites (reserve 1 tablespoon for glaze)
  3 tablespoons sesame seeds
  1 tablespoon butter or margarine, melted

Glaze
    Reserved 1 tablespoon egg white
  1 tablespoon water
  1 teaspoon liquid smoke

Light, crusty buns are flavored with liquid smoke. Great — hot or cold — with any hearty barbecue! Only two hours to prepare these novel "smoky" buns.

50

In large mixer bowl, combine 2 cups of flour, sugar, salt and dry yeast. Add warm water, butter, barbecue seasoning, liquid smoke and egg whites. Blend at low speed until moistened; beat 3 minutes at medium speed. By hand, stir in remaining flour to form a stiff dough. Knead on floured surface until smooth, about 5 minutes. Place in greased bowl, turning to grease top. Cover; let rise in warm place until light and doubled in size, about 1 hour. Prepare Glaze.

Divide dough in half. On floured surface, roll out each portion to a 16x9-inch rectangle. Cut dough lengthwise into three 16x3-inch strips. Cut strips in half, crosswise. Roll up jelly-roll fashion, starting with the 3-inch ends. Pinch edges to seal. Place, seam-side down, on greased cookie sheets. With scissors or sharp knife, make a diagonal cut across top of each bun. Brush tops with Glaze. Sprinkle generously with sesame seeds. Let rise in warm place until light and doubled in size, about 45 minutes. Bake at 400° for 20 to 25 minutes until golden brown. Brush with melted butter. Serve warm or cold.

Glaze: In small mixing bowl, combine reserved egg white, water and liquid smoke.

*For use with Pillsbury's Best Self-Rising Flour, omit salt.

Onion soup mix adds the zest to these rye rounds topped with caraway seed. What a dinner roll with any meat! Or split for interesting hamburger buns. Ready in about two hours.

Onion Rye Rolls

    I envelope dry onion soup mix
    I cup water
    ¾ cup Pillsbury Hungry Jack Mashed
        Potato Flakes
I½ cups rye flour
    I package active dry yeast
    2 tablespoons sugar
    2 tablespoons caraway seed
    2 tablespoons cooking oil
    ⅔ cup evaporated milk
    I egg (slightly beat and reserve I
        tablespoon)
I½ cups Pillsbury's Best All Purpose or
        Self-Rising Flour
    I teaspoon caraway seed

OVEN 375°   I2 ROLLS

In saucepan, combine I cup water with ⅓ cup of the dry onion soup mix; bring to boil. Remove from heat. Add potato flakes; cool. In large mixer bowl, combine rye flour, yeast, sugar and 2 tablespoons caraway seed. Add cooled soup mixture, cooking oil, evaporated milk and egg to dry ingredients. Blend at lowest speed until moistened; beat 3 minutes at medium speed. By hand, stir in flour to form a stiff dough. Knead on floured surface until smooth, about 2 minutes. Place in greased bowl, turning to grease top. Cover; let rest about 30 minutes.

Roll out dough on floured surface to ½-inch thickness. Cut with a 3-inch cookie cutter. Place on greased cookie sheet. Cover; let rise in warm place until doubled in size, about I hour. Brush tops with the reserved egg and sprinkle with remaining onion soup mix combined with I teaspoon caraway seed. Bake at 375° for I5 to 20 minutes. Serve warm.

Tip: In place of cookie cutter, use any can of about 3-inch diameter to cut out rolls.

Bread sticks made savory with dill and chopped chives. Pretty to look at in their speckled garb of coarse salt and caraway seed. Two and a half hours.

Herb Stickles

2½ to 3 cups Pillsbury's Best All Purpose
        Flour*
    I tablespoon sugar
I½ teaspoons salt
    2 tablespoons chopped chives
    2 teaspoons dill seed
    I package active dry yeast
    I cup warm water
    2 tablespoons shortening
    Milk
    Coarse salt
    Caraway seed

OVEN 400°   32 BREAD STICKS

In large mixer bowl, combine I cup of flour, sugar, salt, chives, dill seed and dry yeast. Add warm water and shortening. Blend at lowest speed until moistened; beat 3 minutes at medium speed. By hand, stir in remaining flour to form a stiff dough. Cover; let rise in warm place until light and doubled in size, about I hour.

Toss dough on floured surface until no longer sticky. Divide dough into 4 parts; cut each part into 8 pieces. With floured fingers, roll each piece into strips 8-inches long. Place on greased cookie sheets. Brush with milk, sprinkle on coarse salt and caraway seed. Let rise in warm place until light and doubled in size, 30 to 45 minutes. Bake at 400° for I5 to I8 minutes until golden brown.

*For use with Pillsbury's Best Self-Rising Flour, omit salt in dough.

52

Remember the fun of a porch supper? Bring it back with old-fashioned anise-flavored braided rolls — baked and ready in about 3 hours.

Porch Supper Braids

 3¼ to 3½ cups Pillsbury's Best All Purpose
   Flour*
 3 tablespoons sugar
 2 teaspoons salt
 I teaspoon anise seed, if desired
 I package active dry yeast
 I cup milk
 ¼ cup butter or margarine
 I egg
   Sesame seeds

OVEN 400°   12 TO 18 ROLLS

In large mixing bowl, combine I cup of flour, sugar, salt, anise seed and dry yeast. In saucepan, heat milk and butter until milk is warm. (Butter does not need to melt.) Add egg and warm milk to flour mixture; beat until smooth. Gradually stir in remaining flour to form a stiff dough. Knead on floured surface until smooth and satiny, about 5 minutes. Place in greased bowl, turning to grease top. Cover; let rise in warm place until light and doubled in size, 1½ to 2 hours.

Punch down dough; roll out on lightly floured surface to ½-inch thickness. Cut into 5x1-inch strips. Braid strips together in groups of three; seal ends. Place on greased cookie sheets. Brush tops of rolls with milk or beaten egg; sprinkle with sesame seeds. Cover; let rise in warm place until doubled in size, 30 to 45 minutes. Bake at 400° for 12 to 15 minutes until golden brown.

*For use with Pillsbury's Best Self-Rising Flour, omit salt.

Crunchy-crusted onion twists that will be the hit of your barbecue or spaghetti dinner. Easy-made with mixes in about two hours.

Barbecue Twists

 I package Pillsbury Hot Roll Mix
 4 tablespoons (½ envelope) dry onion
   soup mix
 ¼ cup dairy sour cream
   Poppy or sesame seeds

OVEN 375°   18 ROLLS

Prepare hot roll mix as directed on package, adding 2 tablespoons dry soup mix to water.

After first rise, toss on well-floured surface until no longer sticky. Roll out to an 18x10-inch rectangle. Combine sour cream and remaining 2 tablespoons soup mix. Spread over rectangle. Fold rectangle in half to form an 18x5-inch rectangle. Cut into 1-inch strips. Twist each strip twice and place on greased cookie sheets. Brush twists with milk; sprinkle with poppy or sesame seeds. Cover; let rise until light and doubled in size, 30 to 45 minutes. Bake at 375° for 15 to 18 minutes until golden brown. Serve warm.

Crispy sticks of bread, crisped with caraway and celery seed and just a hint of rye bread flavor. They'll take about 3 hours.

Bit O'Rye Breadsticks

 2¼ to 2¾ cups Pillsbury's Best All Purpose
   Flour*
 I cup rye flour
 I tablespoon sugar
 2 teaspoons salt
 2 teaspoons caraway seed
 ½ teaspoon celery seed
 I package active dry yeast
 2 tablespoons shortening
 I cup warm water
 I egg
   Coarse salt crystals

OVEN 400°   36 BREADSTICKS

In large mixing bowl, combine I cup of flour, rye flour, sugar, salt, caraway seed, celery seed and dry yeast. Add shortening, warm water and egg. Beat until smooth. Stir in remaining flour to form a stiff dough. Knead on floured surface until smooth and elastic, about 5 minutes. Place in greased bowl, turning to grease top. Cover; let rise in warm place until light and doubled in size, 1 to 1½ hours.

Punch down dough; divide into 36 pieces. Shape each piece into an 8-inch long breadstick by rolling between hands. Place on lightly greased cookie sheets. Cover; let rise in warm place until light and doubled in size, about 1 hour. Brush with cold water; sprinkle with coarse salt crystals. Bake at 400° for 15 to 17 minutes until golden brown.

Tip: If desired, omit rye flour and use 3¼ to 3¾ cups all purpose flour.

*For use with Pillsbury's Best Self-Rising Flour, omit salt.

Batter Breads & Rolls

● Not all beautiful breads need be kneaded and shaped. This collection of quick and easy yeast breads are simply spooned into baking dishes. They shape as they bake, and beckon all appetites with their homey, yeast aroma. Herein are recipes for coffeetime, dinnertime or anytime, each made with the soft-dough ease of batter bread. Browse through and plan a batter bread to serve tonight.

Batter yeast dough which is spread in pan with a cocoa-nut mixture on top — plus a rum glaze added after baking. Serve warm in two hours.

Carioca Coffee Cake

    2¼ cups Pillsbury's Best All Purpose Four*
     ¼ cup sugar
      I teaspoon salt
      I package active dry yeast
     ¾ cup milk
     ¼ cup butter or margarine
      I egg

Topping

     ⅓ cup firmly packed brown sugar
      2 tablespoons butter or margarine,
          softened
      I tablespoon flour
      I tablespoon cocoa
     ½ cup chopped walnuts
     ½ teaspoon rum flavoring

Rum Glaze

      2 tablespoons butter or margarine
     ½ cup confectioners' sugar
      I to 2 tablespoons cream
     ½ teaspoon rum flavoring

OVEN 375°   I COFFEE CAKE

In large mixing bowl, combine I cup of flour, sugar, salt and dry yeast. In saucepan, heat milk and butter until milk is warm. (Butter does not need to melt.) Add egg and warm milk to flour mixture. Blend until smooth. Stir in remaining flour; mix thoroughly. Spread in greased 9-inch square pan. Sprinkle with Topping. Cover; let rise in warm place until light and doubled in size, about I hour. Bake at 375° for 30 to 35 minutes until golden brown. While warm, drizzle with Rum Glaze.

Topping: Combine all ingredients and blend until mixture is crumbly.

Rum Glaze: Brown butter in saucepan over medium heat. Add remaining ingredients; beat until smooth.

*For use with Pillsbury's Best Self-Rising Flour, omit salt.

Just three hours to prepare this crusty dill-flavored bread, baked in a round casserole.

Dilly Casserole Bread

    2½ to 3 cups Pillsbury's Best All
          Purpose Flour*
      2 tablespoons sugar
      I tablespoon instant minced onion
      2 teaspoons dill seed
    I¼ teaspoons salt
     ¼ teaspoon soda
      I package active dry yeast
      I cup creamed cottage cheese
     ¼ cup water
      I tablespoon butter or margarine
      I egg
          Butter, softened
          Coarse salt, if desired

OVEN 350°   I ROUND LOAF

In large mixer bowl, combine I cup of flour, sugar, onion, dill seed, salt, soda and dry yeast. In saucepan, heat cottage cheese, water and butter until mixture is warm. Add egg and warm liquid to flour mixture. Blend at lowest speed until moistened; beat 3 minutes at medium speed. By hand, stir in remaining flour to form a stiff dough. Cover; let rise in warm place until light and doubled in size, about I hour.

Stir down dough. Turn into well-greased 8-inch round (I½ or 2 quart) casserole. Cover; let rise in warm place until light, 30 to 45 minutes. Bake at 350° for 35 to 40 minutes until golden brown. Brush with butter and sprinkle with coarse salt, if desired.

*For use with Pillsbury's Best Self-Rising Flour, omit salt and soda.

MENU
Saturday Night Supper
Meat Loaf
Hash Brown Potatoes
Tossed Salad
Dilly Casserole Bread
Cherry Crisp
Beverage

56

Plump, juicy raisins are the surprise in this lemon-flavored bread. Rich caramel-pecan topping glazes rolls or coffee ring — ready in 2½ hours.

Two-Way Coffee Bread

  2 cups Pillsbury's Best All Purpose Flour*
  ½ cup raisins
  2 tablespoons sugar
  ¾ teaspoon salt
  ½ teaspoon grated lemon peel
   1 package active dry yeast
  ½ cup warm water
  ¼ cup butter or margarine, softened
   1 egg

<u>Topping</u>

  ⅓ cup firmly packed brown sugar
  ¼ cup chopped pecans
  2 tablespoons sugar
  ½ teaspoon cinnamon
  2 tablespoons butter or margarine, melted
  2 tablespoons corn syrup
  1 tablespoon water

OVEN 375°   9-INCH COFFEE RING OR 12 ROLLS

In large mixing bowl, combine 1 cup of flour, raisins, sugar, salt, lemon peel and dry yeast. Add warm water, butter and egg. Blend well; beat until smooth. Stir in remaining flour. Cover; let rise in warm place until light and doubled in size, about 1 hour.

Divide Topping among 12 greased muffin cups or place in greased 9-inch ring mold. Stir down dough; divided among muffin cups or spread in ring mold. Cover; let rise in warm place until light and doubled in size, about 45 minutes. Bake at 375° for 18 to 23 minutes until golden brown. Turn out immediately onto cooling racks or serving plate.

<u>Topping</u>: Combine all ingredients.

<u>Tip:</u> *If desired, Coffee Bread may be prepared and shaped a day ahead and allowed to rise in the refrigerator until ready to bake the next day. Shape rolls or ring and place in pans as directed above. Cover and refrigerate until ready to use. Set rolls or coffee cake out on counter about 15 minutes before baking as directed above.*

*For use with Pillsbury's Best Self-Rising Flour, omit salt.

Everything's coming up raves with this colorful candied fruit bread. Quick and easy for holiday entertaining. Allow 3 hours to make and bake.

No-Knead Holiday Bread

  3 to 3½ cups Pillsbury's Best All Purpose Flour*
  ¼ cup sugar
  1½ teaspoons salt
   1 package active dry yeast
   1 cup milk
  ¼ cup shortening
   1 egg
   1 cup chopped mixed candied fruit
  ¾ cup raisins

OVEN 350°   1 LOAF

In large mixing bowl, combine 1 cup of flour, sugar, salt and dry yeast. In saucepan, heat milk and shortening until milk is warm. (Shortening does not need to melt.) Add warm milk and egg to flour mixture. Beat until smooth. Stir in candied fruit and raisins. Gradually stir in remaining flour to form a stiff batter. Turn into greased 9x5-inch loaf pan. Let rise in warm place until light and doubled in size, about 1½ hours. Bake at 350° for 50 to 60 minutes until golden brown.

<u>Tip:</u> *For a spicy Holiday Bread, add ½ teaspoon nutmeg with salt.*

*Pillsbury's Best Self-Rising Flour is not recommended for use in this recipe.

Cheddar cheese, with a zingy hint of cayenne, make these potato-cheese rolls distinctive. Give yourself about three hours.

Tato-Flake Cheese Buns

    3 to 3¼ cups Pillsbury's Best All
      Purpose Flour*
    1 tablespoon sugar
    2 teaspoons salt
    ⅛ teaspoon cayenne pepper
    1 package active dry yeast
    ½ cup Pillsbury Hungry Jack Mashed
      Potato Flakes
    1 cup boiling water
    ¾ cup evaporated milk
    ¼ cup shortening
    1 egg
    1 cup shredded Cheddar cheese

OVEN 375°   24 ROLLS

In large mixer bowl, combine 2 cups of flour, sugar, salt, cayenne pepper, dry yeast and dry potato flakes. Combine boiling water, evaporated milk and shortening; cool to lukewarm. Add egg and warm liquid to flour mixture. Blend at lowest speed until moistened; beat 3 minutes at medium speed. By hand, stir in remaining flour and cheese to form a stiff batter. Cover; let rise in warm place until light and doubled in size, 1 to 1½ hours.

Stir down batter. Spoon batter into 24 well-greased muffin cups. Cover; let rise in warm place until light and doubled in size, 45 to 60 minutes. Bake at 375° for 20 to 25 minutes, until golden brown. Remove from pans immediately.

*For use with Pillsbury's Best Self-Rising Flour, omit salt.

MENU
Ladies' Luncheon
Tomato stuffed with Crabmeat Salad
Tato-Flake Cheese Buns
Relishes
Cheese Cake Pie with
Blueberry Fruit Topping
Beverage

Yeast batter dough pressed into a jelly roll pan topped with slivered almonds and creamy orange marmalade. Only an hour in the kitchen creates this tasty delight.

Almond Marmalettes

    2 to 2½ cups Pillsbury's Best All
      Purpose Flour*
    2 tablespoons sugar
    1 teaspoon salt
    1 package active dry yeast
    ⅔ cup milk
    ⅓ cup shortening
    1 egg
    ½ cup chopped maraschino cherries,
      if desired
    1 cup slivered almonds

<u>Almond Cream</u>
    1 cup confectioners' sugar
    1 cup (12 oz. jar) orange marmalade
    ¼ cup butter or margarine, softened
    ¼ cup cream
    ½ teaspoon vanilla
    ¼ teaspoon almond extract

OVEN 350°   15X10-INCH COFFEE CAKE

In large mixer bowl, combine 1 cup of flour, sugar, salt and dry yeast. In saucepan, heat milk and shortening until milk is warm. (Shortening does not need to melt.) Add egg and warm milk to flour mixture. Blend at low speed until moistened; beat 3 minutes at medium speed. By hand, stir in remaining flour to form a stiff batter. Cover; let rise in warm place until light and doubled in size, 45 to 60 minutes. Stir down batter; press with fingertips into well-greased 15x10-inch jelly roll pan or two 9-inch square pans. Cover; let rise in warm place until light and doubled in size, 20 to 30 minutes. Spoon Almond Cream over dough; spread to cover. Sprinkle with maraschino cherries. Bake at 350° for 15 minutes. Sprinkle with almonds and return to oven for 10 to 15 minutes until golden brown.

<u>Almond Cream</u>: Combine all ingredients; mix well.

*For use with Pillsbury's Best Self-Rising Flour, omit salt.

No kneading required for this light, tender coffee cake that features a crunchy almond-sugar topping. Better yet, it's extra quick and easy.

Sugar Mountain Loaf

    2 eggs (separate I egg and reserve white)
 ½ cup sugar
    I teaspoon salt
    I package active dry yeast
    I tablespoon anise seed, if desired
 ¾ cup milk
 ¼ cup butter or margarine
 2½ cups Pillsbury's Best All Purpose Flour*
 ¼ cup slivered almonds
 ¼ cup sugar

OVEN 350°   I COFFEE CAKE

In large mixer bowl, beat egg, egg yolk and sugar at high speed until thick and light colored. Add salt, dry yeast and anise seed. In saucepan, heat milk and butter until milk is warm. (Butter does not need to melt.) Add warm milk to egg mixture and beat at low speed one minute. By hand, stir in flour to make a stiff batter. Spread dough in well-greased 9 or 10-inch tube pan. Cover; let rise in warm place until light and doubled in size, 1½ to 2 hours. Brush with slightly beaten reserved egg white. Sprinkle on slivered almonds and sugar. Bake at 350° for 35 to 40 minutes until golden brown. Remove from pan; turn right side up and cool.

Tip: I teaspoon lemon extract may be used in place of anise seed.

*For use with Pillsbury's Best Self-Rising Flour, increase flour to 3 cups; omit salt.

Light, honey-flavored dinner rolls ready in about 2½ hours. Made easy from a no-knead batter.

Honey Twin Rolls

 6 to 6¼ cups Pillsbury's Best All
    Purpose Flour*
 2 teaspoons salt
 2 packages active dry yeast
 1¾ cups warm water
 ½ cup honey
 ¼ cup shortening
    I egg

OVEN 400°   36 ROLLS

In large mixer bowl, combine 3 cups of flour, salt and dry yeast. Add warm water, honey, shortening and egg. Blend at lowest speed until moistened; beat I minute at medium speed. By hand, stir in remaining flour to form a stiff batter, mixing until smooth. Cover; let rise in warm place until light and doubled in size, about I hour.

Stir down batter. Using about 2 tablespoons per roll, form twin rolls by dropping into greased muffin cups. Cover; let rise in warm place until light and doubled in size, about 45 minutes. Bake at 400° for I2 to I5 minutes until golden brown.

Tip: For I8 rolls, use ¾ cup warm water, I egg and half of remaining ingredients.

*For use with Pillsbury's Best Self-Rising Flour, omit salt.

MENU
"Spur of the Moment" Supper
Tuna-Cheese Casserole
Potato Chips
Gelatin Fruit Salad
Honey Twin Rolls
Chocolate Cake
Beverage

Rich 'n moist is the name of the game in this tender batter bread. Easy does it, too. Allow close to three hours before you can cut those golden slices.

Golden Cake Bread

    4 to 4½ cups Pillsbury's Best All
      Purpose Flour*
  ½ cup sugar
   I teaspoon salt
   I package active dry yeast
   I cup milk
  ½ cup butter or margarine
   2 eggs
   2 teaspoons vanilla

OVEN 350°   I LARGE LOAF

In large mixer bowl, combine 2 cups of flour, sugar, salt and dry yeast. In saucepan, heat milk and butter until milk is warm. (Butter does not need to melt.) Add eggs, vanilla and warm milk to flour mixture. Mix at lowest speed until moistened; beat 2 minutes at medium speed. By hand, stir in remaining flour to form a stiff batter. Cover; let rise in warm place until light and doubled in size, about I hour.

Stir down batter. Spread in well-greased 9¼ x 5¼-inch loaf pan. Cover; let rise in warm place until light and doubled in size, about 45 minutes. Bake at 350° for 40 to 45 minutes until golden brown. Cool 5 minutes; remove from pan.

<u>Tip</u>: *On humid days, use maximum amount of flour.*

*For use with Pillsbury's Best Self-Rising Flour, use 4½ cups of flour and omit salt.

Batter rolls featuring smoky cheese flavor, shaped in muffin cups in about two hours. Golden buns will enhance your next luncheon — so easy and quick.

Easy Cheesy Buns

 2¼ cups Pillsbury's Best All Purpose Flour*
   2 tablespoons sugar
   I teaspoon salt
   I package active dry yeast
  ½ cup milk
  ⅔ cup diced smoky cheese spread
   2 tablespoons butter or margarine
   I egg

OVEN 375°   I2 ROLLS

In large mixer bowl, combine I cup of flour, sugar, salt and dry yeast. In saucepan, heat milk, cheese spread and butter until milk is warm. (Cheese and butter do not need to melt.) Add egg and warm liquid to flour mixture. Blend at lowest speed until cheese is well blended, about 2 minutes. By hand, stir in remaining flour to form a stiff batter. Divide dough into I2 parts; place in well-greased muffin cups. Cover; let rise in warm place until doubled in size, I to I½ hours. Bake at 375° for I2 to I5 minutes until golden brown. Serve hot.

*For use with Pillsbury's Best Self-Rising Flour, omit salt.

Spicy little batter buns. Moist rolls . . . so easy and ideal for your best luncheons or dinners. Only keeps you in the kitchen for an hour.

Savory Spoon Buns

   3 to 3¼ cups Pillsbury's Best All
      Purpose Flour*
   2 tablespoons sugar
   I teaspoon salt
   I teaspoon caraway seed
  ½ teaspoon ground sage
  ⅛ teaspoon nutmeg
   I package active dry yeast
   I cup milk
   2 tablespoons shortening
   I egg

OVEN 400°   I2 ROLLS

In large mixer bowl, combine I cup of flour, sugar, salt, caraway seed, sage, nutmeg and dry yeast. In saucepan, heat milk and shortening until milk is warm. (Shortening does not need to melt.) Add warm milk and egg to dry ingredients. Mix at low speed until moistened; beat about 2 minutes at medium speed. By hand, stir in remaining flour to form a stiff batter.

Spoon into well-greased muffin cups, filling about ⅔ full. Let rise in warm place until light and well-rounded above muffin cups, about 45 minutes. Bake at 400° for I0 to I2 minutes until golden brown. Serve warm.

*For use with Pillsbury's Best Self-Rising Flour, omit salt.

Candied fruit and nuts make these muffins holiday special. To vary, add semi-sweet chocolate pieces. Easy and quick to make.

Raised Holiday Muffins

3½ to 4 cups Pillsbury's Best All
    Purpose Flour*
 I cup sugar
1½ teaspoons salt
 2 packages active dry yeast
 I cup dairy sour cream
 ⅓ cup water
 ⅓ cup butter or margarine
 3 eggs
 ⅔ cup chopped nuts
 ½ cup chopped candied fruit
    Melted butter
 ½ cup sugar
 ⅓ cup chopped nuts

OVEN 400°   ABOUT 24 MUFFINS

In large mixer bowl, combine I cup of flour, sugar, salt and dry yeast. In saucepan, heat sour cream, water and butter until mixture is warm. (Butter does not need to melt.) Add eggs and warm liquids to flour mixture. Blend at lowest speed until moistened; beat 3 minutes at medium speed. By hand, stir in nuts, candied fruit and remaining flour to form a stiff batter. Fill greased muffin cups about half full. Cover; let rise in warm place until light and doubled in size, I to I½ hours. Carefully brush muffins with melted butter; sprinkle with mixture of sugar and nuts. Bake at 400° for I5 to 20 minutes until light brown. Serve warm.

Tip: I cup (6 oz. package) semi-sweet chocolate pieces may be added with nuts and candied fruit.

*For use with Pillsbury's Best Self-Rising Flour, omit salt.

MENU
"Before-The-Game" Tailgate Party
Barbecued Frankfurters
Potato Chips
Oven Baked Beans
Relishes
Half-Time Spoon Rolls
Savory Spoon Buns
Brownies
Beverage

Take 2½ hours and make these easy-doing dinner rolls. Light, airy batter rolls.

Half-Time Spoon Rolls

3½ cups Pillsbury's Best All Purpose Flour*
 ¼ cup sugar
 I teaspoon salt
 I package active dry yeast
1½ cups milk
 ⅓ cup shortening
 I egg

OVEN 400°   ABOUT I8 ROLLS

In large mixer bowl, combine 2 cups of flour, sugar, salt and dry yeast. In saucepan, heat milk and shortening until milk is warm. (Shortening does not need to melt.) Add egg and warm milk to flour mixture. Blend at lowest speed until moistened. Beat 2 minutes at medium speed. By hand, stir in remaining flour to form a stiff batter. Cover; let rise in warm place until light and doubled in size, 45 to 60 minutes.

Stir down batter. Spoon into greased muffin cups, filling each about half full. Cover; let rise in warm place until light and doubled in size, about 45 minutes. Bake at 400° for I5 to 20 minutes until golden brown.

*For use with Pillsbury's Best Self-Rising Flour, omit salt.

Coffeetime Breads & Rolls

● When the bunch comes for brunch or the crowd comes for coffee, here's your chance to indulge yourself in something sensational. Choose the soft and sticky type, fruited and sweet . . . or perhaps a crunchy crisp that melts in the mouth . . . or maybe this is the moment for the rich-rich roll, layered with butter and crowned with nuts. These coffeetime winners include everything from doughnuts to coffee cakes, from kuchens to sweet rolls. Choose the one that best fits the occasion and serve it with a flourish.

It's a flower of a coffee cake, with cinnamon 'n sugar crusted petals. A pretty serving, ready in three and a half hours, or note the tip to make ahead.

Sweet Petals

2¾ to 3¼ cups Pillsbury's Best All Purpose
   Flour*
2 tablespoons sugar
1½ teaspoons salt
1 package active dry yeast
1 cup milk
3 tablespoons butter or margarine
¾ cup sugar
¼ cup firmly packed brown sugar
2 teaspoons cinnamon
⅓ cup butter or margarine, melted

OVEN 350°   TWO 9-INCH COFFEE CAKES

In large mixer bowl, combine 1½ cups of flour, sugar, salt and dry yeast. In saucepan, heat milk and butter until milk is warm. (Butter does not need to melt.) Add to flour mixture. Blend at lowest speed until moistened. Beat 3 minutes at medium speed. By hand, stir in remaining flour to form a stiff dough. Knead on floured surface until smooth and elastic, 2 to 3 minutes. Place in greased bowl, turning to grease top. Cover; let rise in warm place until light and doubled in size, 1 to 1½ hours.

Punch down dough. Divide into 24 pieces. Shape each piece into a strip about 5 inches long by rolling between hands. Combine sugar, brown sugar and cinnamon. Dip strips in melted butter, then in cinnamon-sugar mixture. Place in 2 greased 9-inch round layer pans, starting in center and winding in coil to outside of pan, forming petals with each piece of dough. Sprinkle any leftover sugar over top of coffee cake. Cover; let rise in warm place until light and doubled in size, 45 to 60 minutes.

Bake at 350° for 25 to 30 minutes until light golden brown. Invert immediately onto cooling rack. Let stand 5 minutes. Turn right-side up onto serving plate. If desired, drizzle with Vanilla Glaze, page 12. Sprinkle with chopped nuts.

Tips: Pillsbury Hot Roll Mix may be used for yeast dough in this recipe. Prepare as directed on package and shape as directed above.

For fresh baked coffee cake the next morning, cover tightly and refrigerate shaped coffee cake. Place in cold oven and set oven temperature at 350°. Bake for 30 to 35 minutes.

*For use with Pillsbury's Best Self-Rising Flour, omit salt.

A festive combination of candied fruits, nuts and jelly in a round and pretty spiral. Give yourself 3 hours.

Merry-Go-Round Coffee Cake

2½ to 3 cups Pillsbury's Best All Purpose
   Flour*
¼ cup sugar
1 teaspoon salt
1 package active dry yeast
¾ cup milk
2 tablespoons shortening
1 egg

Fruit Filling
½ cup favorite jelly
¼ cup chopped mixed candied fruit
¼ cup chopped candied cherries
¼ cup raisins
¼ cup chopped pecans

OVEN 350°   1 COFFEE CAKE

In large mixing bowl, combine 1 cup of flour, sugar, salt and dry yeast. In saucepan, heat milk and shortening until milk is warm. (Shortening does not need to melt.) Blend into flour mixture along with egg. Gradually add remaining flour to form a stiff dough. Knead on floured surface until smooth and elastic, about 3 minutes. Place in greased bowl, turning to grease top. Cover; let rise in warm place until light and doubled in size, about 1 hour.

Roll out to a 20x9-inch rectangle. Spread with Fruit Filling. Roll up, jelly-roll fashion, starting with 20-inch side; seal edges well. Flatten roll slightly; cut lengthwise, dividing roll into two 20-inch strips. Turn cut-sides up. Place one strip on greased cookie sheet. Loosely coil the strip pinwheel fashion, keeping cut edge up. Join second strip to end of first strip and continue winding the dough to make a round coffee cake, about 9 inches in diameter. Cover; let rise in warm place until light and doubled in size, about 45 minutes. Bake at 350° for 25 to 30 minutes until golden brown. While warm, drizzle with Vanilla Glaze, page 12.

Fruit Filling: Combine all ingredients.

Tip: Each strip of dough may be coiled separately and made into two small coffee cakes.

*For use with Pillsbury's Best Self-Rising Flour, omit salt.

Maple Butter Twists

3¼ to 3½ cups Pillsbury's Best All Purpose
    Flour*
  3 tablespoons sugar
1½ teaspoons salt
  1 package active dry yeast
  ¾ cup milk
  ¼ cup butter
  2 eggs

Filling
  ½ cup firmly packed brown sugar
  ⅓ cup sugar
  2 tablespoons flour
  ½ teaspoon cinnamon
  ¼ cup butter, softened
  ¼ cup maple syrup
  ½ teaspoon maple flavoring, if desired
  ½ cup chopped walnuts

OVEN 350°   2 COFFEE CAKES

In large mixer bowl, combine 1½ cups of flour, sugar, salt and dry yeast. In saucepan, heat milk and butter until milk is warm. (Butter does not need to melt.) Add warm milk and eggs to flour mixture. Blend at low speed until moistened; beat 3 minutes at medium speed. By hand, stir in remaining flour to form a stiff dough. Cover; let rise in warm place until light and doubled in size, about 1½ hours. Prepare Filling.

Divide dough in half. Roll out each on floured surface to a 14x8-inch rectangle. Spread each with half of Filling. Roll up, jelly-roll fashion, starting with 14-inch side. Seal edges. Place each roll in a circle in a well-greased 8-inch round layer pan. With scissors or sharp knife, cut rolls in half legthwise. For each coffee cake, twist the two strips together, cut-sides up, sealing ends together. Gently flatten with fingertips. Cover; let rise in warm place until light and doubled in size, about 1 hour. Bake at 350° for 25 to 30 minutes until golden brown. Drizzle with Maple Glaze, page 12, while warm.

Filling: In small mixer bowl, combine all ingredients except walnuts. Beat at medium speed about 2 minutes. Stir in walnuts.

*For use with Pillsbury's Best Self-Rising Flour, omit salt.

Cherry Ring

  1 package Pillsbury Hot Roll Mix
  ¼ cup butter or margarine, melted
  ¾ cup sugar
  1 teaspoon cinnamon
  1 can (1 lb.) pitted sour pie cherries, drained

OVEN 350°   2 COFFEE RINGS

Prepare hot roll mix as directed on package. After first rise, toss on well-floured surface until no longer sticky. Divide in half. Roll out each half on floured surface to a 12x10-inch rectangle. Spread each with melted butter and sprinkle with mixture of sugar and cinnamon. Place half the cherries on each rectangle. Roll up, jelly-roll fashion, starting with 12-inch side; seal edges. Shape each into a ring, seam-side down, in greased 8 or 9-inch round layer pan; seal ends together. With scissors, cut through ring to within 1 inch of bottom at 1-inch intervals. Turn each piece on its side. Cover; let rise in warm place until light and doubled in size, 30 to 45 minutes. Bake at 350° for 30 to 35 minutes until golden brown. Invert *immediately* onto cooling rack. To serve, place right side up on serving plate; drizzle with Vanilla Glaze, page 12, if desired.

Peeking out from the attractive and unusual criss-crossing top is a sugary apple and raisin filling. Four hours . . . and it's good warm or cold.

Raisin Apple Pair

6½ to 7 cups Pillsbury's Best All Purpose
   Flour*
½ cup sugar
2 teaspoons salt
2 packages active dry yeast
1½ cups milk
½ cup butter or margarine
2 eggs

Raisin Apple Filling

2½ cups finely chopped, pared apple
1 cup cut-up raisins or currants
1 cup firmly packed brown sugar
½ teaspoon salt
½ teaspoon cinnamon

OVEN 350°   2 COFFEE CAKES

In large mixer bowl, combine 2 cups of flour, sugar, salt and dry yeast. In saucepan, heat milk and butter until milk is warm. (Butter does not need to melt.) Add warm milk and eggs to flour mixture. Blend at lowest speed until moistened; beat 3 minutes at medium speed. By hand, stir in remaining flour to form a stiff dough. Knead on floured surface until smooth and elastic, about 5 minutes. Place in greased bowl, turning to grease top. Cover; let rise in warm place until light and doubled in size, 1 to 1½ hours. Line 2 cookie sheets with aluminum foil and grease well. Turn up edges to form a rim. Prepare Raisin Apple Filling. Punch down dough; divide in half. Roll out half of dough on floured surface to a 12-inch square. Place on prepared cookie sheet. Spread half of Raisin Apple Filling down center third of dough. Cut dough diagonally at 1-inch intervals on both sides. Fold opposite strips of dough over filling, crossing in center. Seal ends of coffee cake. Repeat process with other half of dough and Filling. Cover; let rise in warm place until light and doubled in size, 45 to 60 minutes. Bake at 350° for 30 to 35 minutes until golden brown. Cool. Drizzle with Vanilla Glaze, page 12.

Raisin Apple Filling: In saucepan, combine all ingredients. Bring to a boil over medium heat. Boil 4 minutes, stirring constantly. Cool.

*Pillsbury's Best Self-Rising Flour is not recommended for use in this recipe.

Light and tender cheese-flavored coffee cake teams well with the apple and raisin filling to make this a most unique coffee cake. Ready in about 3 hours.

Apple Country Coffee Cake

4 to 4½ cups Pillsbury's Best All Purpose
   Flour*
⅓ cup sugar
1 teaspoon salt
2 packages active dry yeast
¼ cup water
1 cup dairy sour cream
½ cup pasteurized process cheese spread
⅓ cup butter or margarine
1 egg

Raisin Nut Topping

1 can (1 lb. 5 oz.) prepared apple pie filling
½ cup raisins
½ cup firmly packed brown sugar
½ cup chopped nuts
¼ teaspoon cinnamon
⅛ teaspoon nutmeg

OVEN 350°   2 COFFEE CAKES

In large mixer bowl, combine 2 cups of flour, sugar, salt and dry yeast. In saucepan, heat water, sour cream, pasteurized process cheese spread and butter, stirring constantly, until mixture is warm. Add to flour mixture along with egg. Blend at lowest speed until moistened; beat 3 minutes at medium speed. By hand, stir in remaining flour to form a stiff dough. Prepare Raisin Nut Topping. Turn dough onto floured surface; knead 10 times. Divide dough in half; roll out one half on floured surface to a 14x10-inch rectangle. Cut into 14 rounds with 2½-inch cutter. Set aside. Combine leftover dough with second half of dough. Press dough into 2 greased 9-inch round layer pans. Spread on Raisin Nut Topping. Arrange rounds in circle on Topping. Let rise until light and doubled in size, about 1½ hours. Bake at 350° for 30 to 35 minutes until golden brown. Cool. Drizzle on Vanilla Glaze, page (12). Cut in wedges and serve with a fork.

Raisin Nut Topping: Combine all ingredients.

*For use with Pillsbury's Best Self-Rising Flour, omit salt.

Creamy orange filling is exposed in layers in this round coffee cake, glazed with marmalade. Ready for coffee klatch in two and a half to three hours.

Marmalade Twist

2½ to 2¾ cups Pillsbury's Best All Purpose
    Flour*
⅓ cup sugar
  I teaspoon salt
  I tablespoon grated orange peel
  I package active dry yeast
½ cup milk
⅓ cup shortening
  I egg
  I teaspoon vanilla
¼ cup orange marmalade

Orange Cream Filling
  I package (3 oz.) cream cheese
  2 tablespoons orange marmalade
  I tablespoon grated orange peel
¼ teaspoon nutmeg
½ cup chopped nuts

OVEN 350°   I COFFEE CAKE

In large mixer bowl, combine I cup of flour, sugar, salt, orange peel and dry yeast. In saucepan, heat milk and shortening until milk is warm. (Shortening does not need to melt.) Add egg, vanilla and warm liquid to flour mixture. Blend at low speed until moistened; beat 3 minutes at medium speed. By hand, stir in remaining flour to form a stiff dough. Cover; let rise in warm place until light and doubled in size, I to I½ hours. Prepare Orange Cream Filling.

Punch down dough. Roll out on floured surface to a 14x12-inch rectangle. Spread with Orange Cream Filling. Starting with 14-inch side, roll up jelly-roll fashion. Place on greased cookie sheet, forming a circle by sealing ends together. With scissors or sharp knife, cut halfway through center of roll all the way around circle, turning cut edge up. With fingertips, flatten slightly. Cover; let rise in warm place until light and doubled in size, 30 to 45 minutes. Bake at 350° for 30 to 40 minutes until deep golden brown. Remove from cookie sheet. While hot, brush with orange marmalade.

Orange Cream Filling: In small mixer bowl, combine all ingredients except nuts; beat until creamy. Stir in nuts.

*For use with Pillsbury's Best Self-Rising Flour, omit salt.

A cinnamon-nut coffee cake, moist and rich with preserves. Pretty as a picture . . . in about three hours.

Peach Flip

5 to 5½ cups Pillsbury's Best All Purpose
    Flour*
½ cup sugar
  2 teaspoons salt
  2 packages active dry yeast
½ cup milk
½ cup butter or margarine
  3 eggs
⅔ cup sugar
  2 teaspoons cinnamon
  I cup chopped nuts
  2 tablespoons butter or margarine, softened
  I cup (I2 oz. jar) peach preserves

OVEN 350°   2 COFFEE CAKES

In large mixer bowl, combine 2 cups of flour, sugar, salt and dry yeast. In saucepan, heat milk and butter until milk is warm. (Butter does not need to melt.) Add warm milk and eggs to flour mixture. Blend at low speed until moistened; beat 3 minutes at medium speed. By hand, stir in remaining flour to form a stiff dough. Knead on floured surface until smooth and satiny, about 5 minutes. Place in greased bowl, turning to grease top. Cover; let rise in warm place until light and doubled in size, I to I½ hours.

In small mixing bowl, combine ⅔ cup sugar, cinnamon and nuts. Divide dough in half. Roll out each portion of dough on floured surface to a 20x10-inch rectangle. Spread each with soft butter and ½ cup peach preserves; sprinkle with sugar-cinnamon mixture. Roll up each jelly-roll fashion starting with 20-inch side. Seal edges and ends. Place seam-side down on greased cookie sheets. Curve each around to make a circle, sealing ends. With scissors or sharp knife, cut about half-way through center of dough all the way around circles. With hand, flatten rolls slightly. Cover; let rise in warm place until light, about 30 minutes. Spread ¼ cup peach preserves on top of each coffee cake. Bake at 350° for 20 to 25 minutes until golden brown. Drizzle with Vanilla Glaze, page I2.

Tip: Substitute orange marmalade or pineapple preserves for the peach preserves.

*For use with Pillsbury's Best Self-Rising Flour, omit salt.

Toasted coconut and orange peel get tucked inside rich sour cream crescents. Then topped with an orange glaze to make this a scrumptious coffee cake. Plan on about 3½ hours to make.

Orange Butter Coffee Cake

2¾ to 3¼ cups Pillsbury's Best All Purpose Flour*
¼ cup sugar
1 teaspoon salt
1 package active dry yeast
¼ cup milk
6 tablespoons butter or margarine
2 eggs
½ cup dairy sour cream
¾ cup sugar
1 cup toasted coconut
2 tablespoons grated orange peel
2 tablespoons butter, melted

Orange Glaze
¼ cup sugar
2 tablespoons orange juice
2 tablespoons butter

OVEN 350°   13X9-INCH COFFEE CAKE

In large mixer bowl, combine 1 cup of flour, sugar, salt and dry yeast. In saucepan, heat milk and butter until milk is warm. (Butter does not need to melt.) Add eggs, sour cream and warm milk to flour mixture. Blend at low speed until moistened; beat 3 minutes at medium speed. By hand, stir in remaining flour to form a stiff dough. Cover; let rise in warm place until light and doubled in size, 1½ to 2 hours. Combine ¾ cup sugar, ¾ cup of toasted coconut and orange peel. Set aside.

Toss dough on well-floured surface until no longer sticky. Divide dough in half. Roll out each part to a 12-inch circle. Brush each with half the melted butter; sprinkle with sugar-coconut mixture. Cut each circle into 12 wedges. Roll up, starting with wide end and roll to point. Place rolls, point-side down, in 3 rows in well-greased 13x9-inch pan. Cover; let rise in warm place until light and doubled in size, 45 to 60 minutes. Bake at 350° for 25 to 30 minutes until golden brown. Pour warm Orange Glaze over warm rolls. Spjrinkle on remaining ¼ cup toasted coconut. Leave in pan until served warm or cold.

Orange Glaze: In saucepan, combine sugar, orange juice and butter. Bring to a boil.

*For use with Pillsbury's Best Self-Rising Flour, omit salt.

A rich, tender orange-flavored coffee cake sure to be a favorite. Plan on about 3 hours from start to finish.

Orange Blossom Coffee Cake

3 to 3½ cups Pillsbury's Best All Purpose Flour*
¼ cup sugar
1 teaspoon salt
1 package active dry yeast
¾ cup milk
¼ cup butter or margarine
1 egg
1 tablespoon grated orange peel
½ cup firmly packed brown sugar
1 teaspoon cinnamon
¼ cup firmly packed brown sugar
1 tablespoon butter or margarine
2 tablespoons orange juice
1 tablespoon grated orange peel
½ cup chopped nuts

OVEN 350°   TWO 9-INCH COFFEE CAKES

In large mixer bowl, combine 1 cup of flour, sugar, salt and dry yeast. In saucepan, heat milk and butter until milk is warm. (Butter does not need to melt.) Add egg, grated orange peel and warm milk to flour mixture. Blend at lowest speed until moistened; beat 3 minutes at medium speed. By hand, stir in remaining flour to form a stiff dough. Cover; let rise in warm place until light and doubled in size, 1 to 1½ hours.

Toss dough on well-floured surface until no longer sticky. Divide dough in half. Roll out each portion to a 15x9-inch rectangle. Combine ½ cup brown sugar and cinnamon. Sprinkle half on each rectangle. Roll up rectangles, starting with 15-inch sides. Place each in a well-greased 8 or 9-inch layer pan, sealing ends together to form a ring. Press down until dough nearly covers all of bottom of pans. With scissors or sharp knife, make slashes almost through dough, 1 inch apart, starting 1 inch from center to within ½ inch of outer edge. Cover; let rise in warm place until light and doubled in size, 45 to 60 minutes. In saucepan, combine ¼ cup brown sugar, butter, orange juice and peel. Bring to a boil; boil one minute. Spread sauce on coffee cakes. Sprinkle each with nuts. Bake at 350° for 30 to 35 minutes until golden brown. Turn out immediately onto cooling racks.

*For use with Pillsbury's Best Self-Rising Flour, omit salt.

Nuts and cherries garnish this pretty Swedish tea ring that holds a surprise fruit combination—pineapple and raisins. Three and one-half hours.

Pineapple Raisin Tea Ring

    5 to 5½ cups Pillsbury's Best All Purpose Flour*
    ½ cup sugar
    2 teaspoons salt
    2 packages active dry yeast
    1¼ cups milk
    ¼ cup shortening
    2 eggs
    ¼ cup butter or margarine, melted
    ⅓ cup firmly packed brown sugar
    2 teaspoons cinnamon
    Chopped nuts
    Maraschino cherries

Pineapple Raisin Filling

    1 can (1 lb. 4 oz.) crushed pineapple, well-drained
    ¾ cup sugar
    1 tablespoon cornstarch
    ½ cup raisins

OVEN 375°   2 TEA RINGS

In large mixer bowl, combine 2 cups of flour, sugar, salt and dry yeast. In saucepan, heat milk and shortening until milk is warm. (Shortening does not need to melt.) Add eggs and warm milk to dry ingredients. Blend at lowest speed until moistened; beat 2 minutes at medium speed. By hand, stir in remaining flour to form a stiff dough. Knead on floured surface until smooth and elastic, about 5 minutes. Place in greased bowl, turning to grease top. Cover; let rise in warm place until light and doubled in size, 1 to 1½ hours. Prepare Filling. Punch down dough. Divide dough in half. Roll out each half on floured surface to a 20x12-inch rectangle. Brush with melted butter. Spread Filling on dough. Combine brown sugar and cinnamon; sprinkle over Filling. Roll up each jelly-roll fashion starting with 20-inch side; seal edges. Shape each into a ring, seam-side down, on greased cookie sheets. With scissors, make cuts 1 inch apart through top of ring to 1 inch from bottom. Alternate cut slices, bringing one to the center and the next to the outside of the ring. Cover; let rise in warm place until light and doubled in size, 45 to 60 minutes. Bake at 375° for 20 to 25 minutes until golden brown. Frost while warm with Vanilla Frosting, page 12. Garnish with nuts and cherries, if desired.

Pineapple Raisin Filling: In saucepan, combine crushed pineapple, sugar and cornstarch. Cook over medium heat until thick. Add raisins; cool.

*For use with Pillsbury's Best Self-Rising Flour, omit salt.

Dazzle them with this giant sunflower, each petal glistening with sweet preserves. So easy with hot roll mix, you need only allow two hours.

Sunflower Coffee Cake

    1 package Pillsbury Hot Roll Mix
    1 tablespoon grated lemon peel
    Preserves

OVEN 375°   1 COFFEE CAKE

Prepare hot roll mix as directed on package, adding lemon peel with flour mixture. After first rise, toss dough on floured surface until no longer sticky. Roll out dough to ½-inch thickness. Cut out doughnuts with doughnut cutter. Arrange doughnut "holes" in center on greased cookie sheet; stretch the doughnuts slightly and place around "holes", petal fashion. Cover; let rise in warm place until light and doubled in size, 45 to 60 minutes. Bake at 375° for 25 to 30 minutes until golden brown. If desired, place 1 teaspoon preserves in center of each petal after baking. Outline petals and center by drizzling with Vanilla Glaze, page 12.

The Danes are famous for this kind of old-world flavor. A swirl of coffee cake with a nutty macaroon-flavored filling, ready in about 3 hours.

Rich Danish Coffee Cake

2½ to 3 cups Pillsbury's Best All Purpose
    Flour*
 3 tablespoons sugar
½ teaspoon salt
 I package active dry yeast
¾ cup butter
¾ cup milk
 I egg, slightly beaten
¼ cup sugar
¼ cup finely chopped almonds

Filling

I¼ cups finely crushed coconut
    macaroons or graham crackers
¼ cup sugar
¼ cup butter or margarine, melted
 I cup cut-up dates or raisins

OVEN 375°   2 COFFEE CAKES

In large mixing bowl, combine 2 cups of flour, sugar, salt and dry yeast. Cut in butter until mixture is crumbly. In saucepan, heat milk until warm. Add to flour mixture along with egg (reserve I tablespoon egg for topping). Mix well. Stir in remaining flour to form a stiff dough. Knead on floured surface until smooth, about 3 minutes. Place in greased bowl, turning to grease top. Cover; let rise in warm place until light and doubled in size, I to I½ hours. Divide dough in half. Roll one half with hands into a 24-inch long roll. With rolling pin, flatten roll until 6 inches wide. Spread half of Filling down center of strip; fold both sides to center and seal well with fingers. Shape into a coil or pretzel on greased cookie sheet. Repeat with remaining dough and Filling. Cover; let rest in warm place 20 to 30 minutes. Blend the reserved beaten egg with I tablespoon water. Brush top of coffee cakes. Combine sugar and almonds. Sprinkle on top of coffee cakes. Bake at 375° for 25 to 30 minutes until golden brown. Remove from cookie sheets; cool.

Filling: In small mixing bowl, combine macaroon crumbs, sugar and butter. Mix well. Stir in dates.

*For use with Pillsbury's Best Self-Rising Flour, omit salt.

Rich coconut filling enhances this moist coffee ring. Wait for the compliments when you serve this. Allow about two and a half hours, or freeze one coffee ring ahead for quick use.

Hawaiian Coffee Ring

3½ to 4 cups Pillsbury's Best All Purpose
    Flour*
¼ cup sugar
 I teaspoon salt
 I package active dry yeast
½ cup evaporated milk
½ cup warm water
 2 eggs

Filling

⅔ cup sugar
½ cup butter or margarine, softened
½ cup flaked coconut
½ cup chopped nuts
½ teaspoon cinnamon
 2 tablespoons evaporated milk
 I teaspoon vanilla

Glaze

I½ cups confectioners' sugar
¼ cup chopped nuts
½ teaspoon vanilla
 2 to 3 tablespoons evaporated milk

OVEN 350°   2 COFFEE CAKES

In large mixer bowl, combine 2 cups of flour, sugar, salt and dry yeast. Add evaporated milk, water and eggs. Mix at low speed until dry ingredients are moistened; beat 3 minutes at medium speed. By hand, stir in remaining flour to form a stiff dough. Knead on floured surface until smooth, about 5 minutes. Place in greased bowl, turning to grease top. Cover; let rise in warm place until light and doubled in size, about 45 minutes. Prepare Filling.

Divide dough in quarters. Press one portion into bottom and up sides of well-greased 9-inch round layer pan. Top with half of Filling. Roll or press out another portion to a 6-inch circle. Place on top of Filling; seal edges. Repeat process with other two portions. Cover; let rise in warm place until light and doubled in size, about 45 minutes. Bake at 350° for 25 to 30 minutes until golden brown. Spread with Glaze while warm.

Filling: In mixing bowl, combine all ingredients.

Glaze: In mixing bowl, combine all ingredients until of spreading consistency.

*For use with Pillsbury's Best Self-Rising Flour, omit salt.

A rich almond topping crunches up during baking on these coffee cakes. Follow tip and make them cream-filled with vanilla pudding, almond-flavored. Serve to those with a sweet tooth, in just an hour and a half.

Crunchy Cream-Filled Kuchen

2¼ to 2½ cups Pillsbury's Best All Purpose
    Flour*
2 tablespoons sugar
I teaspoon salt
¼ teaspoon nutmeg
I package active dry yeast
½ cup milk
2 tablespoons butter or margarine
I egg

Topping
  ½ cup sugar
  ¼ cup butter or margarine
  I tablespoon milk
  ¾ cup slivered almonds

OVEN 375°   2 COFFEE CAKES

In large mixer bowl, combine I cup of flour, sugar, salt, nutmeg and dry yeast. In saucepan, heat milk and butter until milk is warm. (Butter does not need to melt.) Add warm milk and egg to dry ingredients. Mix at low speed until moistened; beat 3 minutes at medium speed. By hand, stir in remaining flour to form a stiff dough. Knead on floured surface until smooth and satiny, about 3 minutes. Press dough into 2 greased 8-inch round layer pans. Cover; let rise until doubled in size, 45 to 60 minutes. Prepare Topping. Spread half of Topping on each coffee cake. Bake at 375° for 20 to 25 minutes until golden brown. Serve warm, cut in squares.

Topping: In saucepan, combine sugar, butter and milk. Heat until sugar dissolves. Add almonds. Cool.

Tips: For extra quick coffee cakes, prepare Pillsbury Hot Roll Mix as directed on package, pressing into two greased 8-inch layer pans. Prepare Topping and spread on coffee cakes just before baking.

For cream-filled kuchen, prepare I package (3¾ oz.) vanilla pudding mix as directed on package, adding ¼ teaspoon nutmeg. After cooking, stir in ¼ teaspoon almond extract. Cool. Split the two coffee cakes in half crosswise and spread half of filling on bottom layer of each. Place top layers over filling.

*For use with Pillsbury's Best Self-Rising Flour, omit salt.

A frosted delight made in a tube pan. Rich coffee cake with a luscious caramel-nut filling that takes only 3½ hours to make.

Topsy-Turvy Coffee Ring

Coffee Ring
  3 to 3¼ cups Pillsbury's Best All Purpose
     Flour*
  ⅓ cup sugar
  1½ teaspoons salt
    I package active dry yeast
  ¾ cup buttermilk
  ¼ cup shortening
  2 eggs

Filling
  ¼ cup butter or margarine, softened
  ⅓ cup firmly packed brown sugar
  I teaspoon cinnamon
  ¾ cup raisins
  ⅓ cup chopped walnuts

OVEN 350°   9-INCH COFFEE RING

Coffee Ring: In large mixer bowl, combine I cup of flour, sugar, salt and dry yeast. In saucepan, heat buttermilk and shortening until buttermilk is warm. (Shortening does not need to melt.) Add eggs and warm liquid to flour mixture. Beat until smooth. Stir in remaining flour to form a stiff dough. Cover; let rise in warm place until light and doubled in size, 1½ to 2 hours.

Punch down dough; roll out on floured surface to a 20x12-inch rectangle. Spread with softened butter; sprinkle with Filling mixture. Roll up, starting with 20-inch side. Cut into 2-inch slices. Arrange slices, cut-side down, in greased 9-inch tube pan. Cover; let rise in warm place until light and doubled in size, 30 to 45 minutes. Bake at 350° for 35 to 45 minutes until golden brown. Drizzle while warm with Vanilla Glaze, page 12.

Filling: In small mixing bowl, combine all ingredients.

*For use with Pillsbury's Best Self-Rising Flour, omit salt.

The perfect Valentine; the memorable table-piece at the shower. Fragrant and nut-crusted, ready from your oven in about three hours.

Sweetheart Coffee Cake

4 to 4½ cups Pillsbury's Best All Purpose
  Flour*
⅓ cup sugar
2 teaspoons salt
2 packages active dry yeast
1 cup milk
⅓ cup butter or margarine
2 eggs
¼ cup butter or margarine, melted
1 cup sugar
1 cup chopped nuts
2 teaspoons cinnamon

OVEN 350°   2 COFFEE CAKES

In large mixer bowl, combine 1½ cups of flour, sugar, salt and dry yeast. In saucepan, heat milk and butter until milk is warm. (Butter does not need to melt.) Add eggs and warm milk to flour mixture. Blend at lowest speed until moistened; beat 3 minutes at medium speed. By hand, stir in remaining flour to form a stiff dough. Knead on floured surface until smooth and elastic, 2 to 3 minutes. Place in greased bowl, turning to grease top. Cover; let rise in warm place until light and doubled in size, about 1 hour.

Punch down dough; divide in half. Roll out each half on floured surface to a 15x10-inch rectangle. Brush each with butter; sprinkle with mixture of sugar, nuts and cinnamon. Roll up each, jelly-roll fashion, starting with 15-inch side. Place each, seam-side up, on greased cookie sheet. Fold half the roll over on top of other half, sealing ends together. Starting at folded end, cut with scissors down center of roll to within 1 inch of other end. Turn the cut halves out, cut-side up, to form a heart. Cover; let rise in warm place until light and doubled in size, about 1 hour. Bake at 350° for 18 to 20 minutes until golden brown.

*For use with Pillsbury's Best Self-Rising Flour, omit salt.

Triple-topped "delish" coffee cake . . . cherry pie filling, sour cream and rich crumb toppings. Serve this one with a fork. Ready after about three hours.

European Coffee Cake

  2 to 2½ cups Pillsbury's Best All Purpose Flour*
  ⅓ cup sugar
  1½ teaspoons salt
  2 packages active dry yeast
  ¾ cup milk
  ¼ cup shortening
  I egg
  ½ teaspoon almond extract
  I can (I lb. 5 oz.) prepared cherry pie filling

Sour Cream Topping
  ½ cup dairy sour cream
  I egg
  2 tablespoon sugar
  ½ teaspoon almond extract
  ⅛ teaspoon salt

Crumb Topping
  I cup Pillsbury's Best All Purpose or Self-Rising Flour
  ¼ cup sugar
  ½ cup butter or margarine, softened

OVEN 350°   2 COFFEE CAKES

In large mixer bowl, combine I cup of flour, sugar, salt and dry yeast. In saucepan, heat milk and shortening until milk is warm. (Shortening does not need to melt.) Add warm milk, egg and almond extract to flour mixture. Blend at low speed until moistened; beat 3 minutes at medium speed. By hand, stir in remaining flour to form a stiff dough. Cover; let rise in warm place until light and doubled in size, about 1½ hours. Prepare Toppings.

Punch down dough; divide in half. Press each half of dough into a greased 9-inch square pan. Spread half of pie filling over each dough. Drizzle Sour Cream Topping over cherries. Sprinkle with Crumb Topping. Let rise in warm place until light and doubled in size, about 30 minutes. Bake at 350° for 35 to 45 minutes until edges are golden brown.

Sour Cream Topping: In small mixing bowl, combine all ingredients.

Crumb Topping: In small mixing bowl, combine flour and sugar. Cut in butter until mixture is crumbly.

Tip: For a different flavored coffee cake, use blueberry or apple pie filling instead of cherry pie filling.

*For use with Pillsbury's Best Self-Rising Flour, omit salt.

A quick 'n easy yeast coffeecake that's ready in 2 hours. Pear or apricot halves peek from beneath the gooey caramel topping.

Swedish Ripple Coffee Cake

  2 to 2¼ cups Pillsbury's Best All Purpose Flour*
  ¼ cup sugar
  ½ teaspoon salt
  I package active dry yeast
  ½ cup milk
  2 tablespoons shortening
  I egg
  I tablespoon butter or margarine, melted
  I can (I lb. 14 oz.) pear or apricot halves, drained

Topping
  I cup firmly packed brown sugar
  ½ cup dairy sour cream
  I tablespoon flour
  ½ teaspoon vanilla

OVEN 350°   I COFFEE CAKE

In medium mixing bowl, combine I cup of flour, sugar, salt and dry yeast. In small saucepan, heat milk and shortening until milk is warm. (Shortening does not need to melt.) Add egg and warm milk to flour mixture. Beat until smooth. Stir in remaining flour to form a stiff dough. With floured fingers, press dough into greased 13x9-inch pan. Brush with melted butter. Cover; let rise in warm place until light and doubled in size, about I hour. Arrange fruit over top of dough; pour Topping over fruit. Bake at 350° for 30 to 35 minutes until Topping is golden brown. Serve warm, cut in squares.

Topping: In small mixing bowl, combine all ingredients. Blend well.

*For use with Pillsbury's Best Self-Rising Flour, omit salt.

A braided ring of coffee cake plumped full of nuts and fruits. Note that preserves can be used for citron. Top with the "snow" of confectioners' sugar in 2½ hours.

Snow Ring

 4 to 4½ cups Pillsbury's Best All Purpose
      Flour*
 1 cup confectioners' sugar
1½ teaspoons salt
 1 package active dry yeast
 1 cup milk
 ½ cup butter or margarine
 2 eggs (reserve one white)
 ½ cup chopped almonds
 ½ cup diced citron
 ½ cup currants
 1 reserved egg white
 1 tablespoon water
 ¼ cup chopped almonds

OVEN 350° 1 LARGE COFFEE CAKE

In large mixing bowl, combine 2 cups of flour, confectioners' sugar, salt and dry yeast. In saucepan, heat milk and butter until milk is warm. (Butter does not need to melt.) Add warm milk and eggs to flour mixture. Blend until smooth. Stir in remaining flour to form a stiff dough. Cover; let rise in warm place until light and doubled in size, about 1 hour.

Punch down dough; divide into 3 equal parts. Shape each into an 18-inch strip. Lay strips on lightly floured surface; flatten slightly. Place the ½ cup chopped almonds down center of one strip, the diced citron down center of next strip and the currants down center of last strip. Seal fillings in dough by pinching edges together. Place on greased cookie sheet. Braid the 3 strips of dough; shape into a ring by sealing ends together. Combine egg white and water; brush over dough. Sprinkle ¼ cup almonds over top. Cover; let rise until light and doubled in size, 30 to 45 minutes. Bake at 350° for 30 to 35 minutes until golden brown. While warm, sprinkle with confectioners' sugar.

Tip: ½ cup apricot preserves or other favorite preserves may be substituted for diced citron.

*For use with Pillsbury's Best Self-Rising Flour, omit salt.

A buttery cinnamon layer swirls in this rich orange loaf. What a prize for breakfast or brunch! Serve warm or toasted . . . three and a half hours does it.

Cinnamon Swirl Orange Loaf

5½ to 6 cups Pillsbury's Best All Purpose
      Flour*
 ⅓ cup sugar
 ¼ cup grated orange peel
 3 teaspoons salt
 ¼ teaspoon soda
 2 packages active dry yeast
 ½ cup milk
 ¼ cup butter or margarine
 1 egg
 ¾ cup orange juice
 1 tablespoon butter or margarine, melted
 ⅓ cup sugar
 3 teaspoons cinnamon

OVEN 350° 2 LOAVES

In large mixer bowl, combine 2½ cups of flour, sugar, orange peel, salt, soda and dry yeast. In saucepan, heat milk and butter until milk is warm. (Butter does not need to melt.) Add warm milk, egg and orange juice to dry ingredients. Blend at low speed until moistened; beat 3 minutes at medium speed. By hand, stir in remaining flour to form a stiff dough. Knead on floured surface until smooth and satiny, about 5 minutes. Place in greased bowl, turning to grease top. Cover; let rise in warm place until light and doubled in size, about 1½ hours.

Divide dough in half. Roll out each half on floured surface to a 20x7-inch rectangle. Brush each with melted butter. Combine sugar and cinnamon; sprinkle half over each rectangle. Roll up each jelly-roll fashion starting with 7-inch side. Seal edges and ends. Place, seam-side down, in 2 well-greased 9x5-inch loaf pans. Cover; let rise in warm place until light and doubled in size, 1 to 1½ hours. Bake at 350° for 40 to 45 minutes until golden brown. Brush with butter.

Tips: For higher loaves, shape dough into 20x6-inch rectangles before rolling up. Place in two 8x4-inch loaf pans.

For a sugary crust, reserve ⅓ of cinnamon-sugar filling. Brush the baked loaves with melted butter and sprinkle with reserved cinnamon-sugar mixture.

*For use with Pillsbury's Best Self-Rising Flour, omit salt and soda.

Scrumptious coconut and pecan filling tucked away in a roll-up style loaf and baked to nut-brown perfection in about 4 hours. Delicious warm or cold.

Old-Fashioned Nut Loaf

2½ to 2¾ cups Pillsbury's Best All Purpose
   Flour*
¼ cup sugar
1½ teaspoons salt
   1 package active dry yeast
¾ cup milk
¼ cup butter or margarine
   2 egg yolks (reserve whites)

Nut Filling
   2 egg whites
   2 tablespoons sugar
¼ teaspoon nutmeg
¾ cup finely chopped pecans
¾ cup flaked coconut

OVEN 350°   1 LOAF

In large mixing bowl, combine 1 cup of flour, sugar, salt and dry yeast. In saucepan, heat milk and butter until milk is warm. (Butter does not need to melt.) Add to flour mixture along with egg yolks. Gradually add remaining flour, mixing well. Cover; let rise in warm place until light and doubled in size, about 2 hours.

Punch down dough; roll out on floured surface to a 12x9-inch rectangle. Spread with Nut Filling. Roll up, starting with 9-inch side. Seal edge and ends. Place seam-side down in greased 9x5-inch loaf pan. Cover; let rise in warm place until light and doubled in size, about 1½ hours. Brush with milk; sprinkle with 1 tablespoon sugar. Bake at 350° for 40 to 45 minutes until golden brown.

Nut Filling: In small mixing bowl, beat egg whites slightly. Stir in remaining ingredients, mixing well.

*For use with Pillsbury's Best Self-Rising Flour, omit salt.

A rich, buttery roll, like Danish pastry. Center is filled with preserves for variety.

Danish Butter Rolls

5 to 5½ cups Pillsbury's Best All Purpose
   Flour*
⅓ cup sugar
   1 teaspoon salt
   2 packages active dry yeast
   1 cup milk
¾ cup butter or margarine
   2 eggs
   1 teaspoon vanilla
¼ cup butter or margarine, softened
      Preserves

Filling
¼ cup firmly packed brown sugar
   1 teaspoon cinnamon
¼ cup chopped pecans

OVEN 400°   24 ROLLS

In large mixer bowl, combine 2 cups of flour, sugar, salt and dry yeast. In saucepan, heat milk and butter until milk is warm. (Butter does not need to melt.) Add eggs, vanilla and warm milk to flour mixture. Blend at lowest speed until moistened; beat 3 minutes at medium speed. By hand, stir in remaining flour to form a stiff dough. Knead on floured surface until smooth and elastic, about 3 minutes. Cover; let stand while preparing Filling.

Roll out dough to a 24x12-inch rectangle. Spread with soft butter; sprinkle on Filling. Roll up jelly-roll fashion, starting with 24-inch side. Cut into 1-inch slices. Place, cut-side down, on well-greased cookie sheets, 3 to 4 inches apart. Flatten to ½-inch thickness. Make depression in center of each; fill with 1 teaspoon of preserves. Cover; let rise in warm place until light and doubled in size, 30 to 45 minutes. Bake at 400° for 10 to 12 minutes until golden brown. Cool. Drizzle with Vanilla Glaze, page 12, if desired.

Filling: In small mixing bowl, combine brown sugar, cinnamon and pecans.

*For use with Pillsbury's Best Self-Rising Flour, omit salt.

Maple-Nut Cinnamon Rolls

    3 to 3½ cups Pillsbury's Best All Purpose
      Flour*
    1 cup quick-cooking rolled oats
    ⅓ cup firmly packed brown sugar
    1½ teaspoons salt
    1 package active dry yeast
    1 cup milk
    ½ cup shortening
    2 eggs
    2 tablespoons butter or margarine, melted

Filling

    ⅔ cup firmly packed brown sugar
    1 tablespoon grated orange peel
    1 teaspoon cinnamon

Topping

    ½ cup maple-flavored syrup
    ¼ cup firmly packed brown sugar
    ¼ cup butter or margarine, softened
    ¼ teaspoon maple flavoring
    ⅔ cup chopped walnuts

OVEN 350°   24 ROLLS

In large mixer bowl, combine 1½ cups of flour, rolled oats, brown sugar, salt and dry yeast. In saucepan, heat milk and shortening until milk is warm. (Shortening does not need to melt.) Add warm milk and eggs to flour mixture. Blend at low speed until moistened; beat 3 minutes at medium speed. By hand, stir in remaining flour to form a stiff dough. Cover; let rise in warm place until doubled in size, about 1½ hours.

Prepare Filling and Topping. Punch down dough; roll out on floured surface to a 24x12-inch rectangle. Brush with melted butter; sprinkle with Filling. Roll up, starting with 24-inch side. Cut into 1-inch slices. Place in prepared pan. Cover; let rise in warm place until light and doubled in size, about 1 hour. Bake at 350° for 30 to 35 minutes until golden brown. Cool 1 minute; invert onto serving plate or wire rack.

Filling: In small mixing bowl, combine all ingredients.

Topping: In small mixing bowl, combine all ingredients; spread in bottom of greased 13x9-inch pan.

Tip: Rolls may be placed in 24 greased muffin cups. Prepare as above, using three walnut halves in bottom of each cup with Topping, omitting chopped walnuts. Bake 25 to 30 minutes.

*For use with Pillsbury's Best Self-Rising Flour, omit salt.

82

Potato flakes make these rolls light and moist. Rich dough rolled in butter and cinnamon-sugar mixture and twisted into "figure 8's" . . . only three hours to sugary yummies!

Butterflier "8's"

1¼ cups hot water
¼ cup butter or margarine
½ cup Pillsbury Hungry Jack Mashed
    Potato Flakes
4 to 4½ cups Pillsbury's Best All Purpose
    Flour*
⅓ cup instant nonfat dry milk
¼ cup sugar
2 teaspoons salt
I package active dry yeast
I egg
½ cup butter or margarine, melted
½ cup sugar
½ cup firmly packed brown sugar
2 teaspoons cinnamon

OVEN 375°   24 ROLLS

In saucepan, heat water and butter to boiling; add potato flakes. Cool to lukewarm. In large mixer bowl, combine 2 cups of flour, dry milk, sugar, salt and dry yeast. Add cooled potato mixture and egg to dry ingredients; blend at low speed until moistened. Beat 3 minutes at medium speed. By hand, stir in remaining flour to form a stiff dough. Knead on floured surface until smooth and satiny, about 5 minutes. Place in greased bowl, turning to grease top. Cover; let rise in warm place until light and doubled in size, I to I½ hours.

Divide dough into four parts. Divide each part into sixths. Roll each piece with palm of hand into an 8-inch strip. Dip each strip in melted butter. Combine sugar, brown sugar and cinnamon; roll strips in sugar mixture. Twist several times and form into figure "8's" on greased cookie sheets. Flatten with palm of hand, shaping to resemble "butterflies". Cover; let rise in warm place until light and doubled in size, about 30 minutes. Bake at 375° for 12 to 15 minutes until golden brown.

Tips: If desired, make an indentation in center of each "butterfly" before baking, and fill with ½ teaspoon jam or preserves.

Substitute I cup milk for instant nonfat dry milk and water, if desired.

*For use with Pillsbury's Best Self-Rising Flour, omit salt.

Captivate the coffee klatch with succulent cin-namon-sugar crusted break apart rolls. Make your own in 3 hours or be quick with the refrigerated dough tip.

Coffee-Time Cinnamon Rolls

3 to 3¼ cups Pillsbury's Best All Purpose
    Flour*
2 tablespoons sugar
I teaspoon salt
I package active dry yeast
1¼ cups milk
2 tablespoons shortening
⅓ cup butter or margarine, melted
⅔ cup sugar
1½ teaspoons cinnamon

OVEN 375°   2 COFFEE CAKES

In large mixer bowl, combine 1½ cups flour, sugar, salt and dry yeast. In saucepan, heat milk and shortening until milk is warm. (Shortening does not need to melt.) Add to flour mixture. Blend at lowest speed until moistened; beat 2 minutes at medium speed. By hand, stir in remaining flour to form a stiff dough. Knead on well-floured surface until smooth and satiny, about 3 minutes. Place in greased bowl, turning to grease top. Cover; let rise in warm place until light and doubled in size, about I hour.

Punch down dough; roll out on floured surface to ½-inch thickness. Cut into rounds with floured 2-inch cutter. Dip each round in melted butter, then in mixture of sugar and cinnamon. Reserve 6 rounds for center of each pan. Arrange remaining rounds, overlapping edges, around sides of two greased 8 or 9-inch round layer pans. Place the 6 reserved rounds in center of each pan. Cover; let rise in warm place until light and doubled in size, about 45 minutes. Bake at 375° for 25 to 30 minutes until golden brown. If desired, drizzle with Vanilla Glaze, page I2. Serve warm or cold.

Tip: For an even easier coffee cake, substitute I can Pillsbury Refrigerated Quick Parkerhouse Dinner Rolls for yeast rolls. Separate each roll into 2 rounds. Dip unbuttered side in 2 tablespoons melted butter, then in mixture of ⅓ cup sugar and ¾ teaspoon cinnamon. Arrange in one 8-inch round layer pan as directed above. Bake at 375° for 25 to 30 minutes.

*For use with Pillsbury's Best Self-Rising Flour, omit salt.

Moist, rich, break-apart cinnamon rolls in four hours. Attractively twisted shape, baked in a bunch in cake pan . . . serve warm or cold.

Frosty Cinnamon Twisters

3 to 3½ cups Pillsbury's Best All Purpose Flour*
¼ cup sugar
1½ teaspoons salt
1 package active dry yeast
¾ cup milk
¼ cup butter or margarine
1 egg
1 teaspoon vanilla
3 tablespoons butter or margarine, melted
¼ cup chopped nuts

Filling

1 cup firmly packed brown sugar
2 teaspoons cinnamon

OVEN 375°   1 COFFEE CAKE

In large mixer bowl, combine 1½ cups of flour, sugar, salt and dry yeast. In saucepan, heat milk and butter until milk is warm. (Butter does not need to melt.) Add warm liquid, egg and vanilla to flour mixture. Mix at low speed until moistened; beat 3 minutes at medium speed. By hand, stir in remaining flour to form a stiff dough. Knead on floured surface until smooth, about 2 minutes. Place in greased bowl, turning to grease top. Cover; let rise in warm place until doubled in size, about 1½ hours. Prepare Filling.

Divide dough into 4 parts. Roll each part to a 12x6-inch rectangle. Brush each with ½ tablespoon melted butter and sprinkle with ¼ of Filling mixture. Roll up, starting with 12-inch side; seal edges and ends. Place the four rolls, one inch apart, in well-greased 13x9-inch pan. With scissors or sharp knife, make slashes almost through rolls at ¾-inch intervals. Turn cut pieces on sides, alternating direction each piece is turned. Brush with remaining 1 tablespoon melted butter and sprinkle with reserved Filling mixture. Cover; let rise in warm place

until light, about 1 hour. Bake at 375° for 20 to 25 minutes until golden brown. Drizzle with Vanilla Glaze, page 12. Sprinkle with chopped nuts.

Filling: Combine sugar and cinnamon. Reserve 3 tablespoons for topping.

*For use with Pillsbury's Best Self-Rising Flour, omit salt.

Easy caramel rolls in only a little over an hour. Looks like you've been at work for hours! Serve 'em hot from the oven . . . and make plenty.

Quick Praline Rolls

2½ to 3 cups Pillsbury's Best All Purpose Flour*
¼ cup sugar
2 teaspoons baking powder
½ teaspoon salt
1 package active dry yeast
⅔ cup warm water
⅓ cup butter or margarine, softened
1 egg
⅓ cup butter or margarine, softened
¾ cup firmly packed brown sugar
¾ cup chopped nuts

OVEN 425°   15 ROLLS

In large mixer bowl, combine 1 cup of flour, sugar, baking powder, salt and dry yeast. Add warm water, butter and egg. Blend at low speed until moistened; beat 3 minutes at medium speed. By hand, stir in remaining flour to form a stiff dough. Set aside. In small mixing bowl, combine butter and brown sugar; blend until creamy.

Roll out dough on well-floured surface to a 15x10-inch rectangle. Spread ⅔ of brown sugar mixture over dough. (Reserve remaining third.) Sprinkle with ½ cup of nuts. Roll up jelly-roll fashion, starting with 15-inch side. Cut into 1-inch slices. Place 3 inches apart on greased cookie sheets. Flatten with fingertips to ½-inch thickness. Spread reserved brown sugar mixture over tops of rolls. Sprinkle with remaining chopped nuts. Cover; let rise in warm place until light and doubled in size, 30 to 45 minutes. Bake at 425° for 10 to 12 minutes until golden brown. Serve warm.

*For use with Pillsbury's Best Self-Rising Flour, omit baking powder and salt.

(Frosty Cinnamon Twisters) Turn cut pieces on sides, alternating direction each piece is turned.

Double nutty, with real chopped nuts plus the nutty flavor of whole wheat. Caramel roll slices, baked in a bunch, are ready in three hours from "go".

Whole Wheat Caramel Rolls

1⅓ cups whole wheat flour
3 tablespoons sugar
1 teaspoon salt
1 package active dry yeast
1 cup milk
2 tablespoons butter or margarine
1 to 1¼ cups Pillsbury's Best All Purpose Flour*
¼ cup butter or margarine, melted
⅔ cup firmly packed brown sugar
½ cup chopped nuts

OVEN 350°   16 ROLLS

In large mixer bowl, combine whole wheat flour, sugar, salt, and dry yeast. In saucepan, heat milk and butter until milk is warm. (Butter does not need to melt.) Add to flour mixture. Blend at lowest speed until moistened; beat 2 minutes at medium speed. By hand, stir in all purpose flour to form a stiff dough. Knead on floured surface until smooth, 2 to 3 minutes. Place in greased bowl, turning to grease top. Cover; let rise in warm place until light and doubled in size, about 1 hour.

Punch down dough; roll out on floured surface to a 16x12-inch rectangle. Spread with melted butter; sprinkle with brown sugar and nuts. Roll up jelly-roll fashion, starting with 16-inch side. Cut into 1-inch slices. Place cut-side down in greased 9-inch square pan. Cover; let rise in warm place until light and doubled in size, about 45 minutes. Bake at 350° for 25 to 30 minutes until golden brown. Invert immediately onto serving plate or cooling rack.

*For use with Pillsbury's Best Self-Rising Flour, omit salt.

MENU
Quick Sunday Morning Breakfast
Fruit Cup
Whole Wheat Caramel Rolls
Beverage

Pecans on the bottom, honey-butter on top, make these tender oblongs good any way you look at them. Eat 'em warm and wonderful in three hours.

Honey Fingers

1 package Pillsbury Hot Roll Mix
¾ cup warm water
1 egg
½ cup Pillsbury Hungry Jack Mashed Potato Flakes
⅓ cup honey
½ cup chopped pecans
¼ cup butter or margarine, melted

Honey Topping
⅓ cup sugar
⅓ cup honey
¼ cup butter or margarine, softened
½ teaspoon cinnamon

OVEN 350°   36 SMALL ROLLS

In large mixing bowl, soften yeast from hot roll mix in warm water. Add egg, potato flakes and honey. Stir to blend. Add flour mixture from hot roll mix and mix well. Cover; let rise in warm place until light and doubled in size, 45 to 60 minutes.

Punch down dough. Roll out on well-floured surface to a 14x6-inch rectangle. Cut into three 14x2-inch rectangles. Cut rectangles crosswise into 12 strips each. Place strips in 13x9-inch pan that has been greased and sprinkled with chopped pecans. Brush on melted butter; spread on Honey Topping. Let rise in warm place until light and doubled in size, 30 to 45 minutes. Bake at 350° for 35 to 40 minutes until golden brown. Turn out of pan immediately.

Honey Topping: In small mixing bowl, combine sugar, honey, butter and cinnamon; mix well.

Richer than rich are these coiled rolls filled with moist frosting, nuts and coconut. So easy with hot roll mix — just two and a half hours.

Nutty Buttercups

    1 package Pillsbury Hot Roll Mix
    ½ cup dairy sour cream
    ¼ cup butter or margarine, softened
    1 package one layer size Pillsbury Buttercream Vanilla Frosting Mix
    1 cup finely chopped macadamia nuts or pecans
    1 cup flaked coconut

OVEN 425°   24 ROLLS

Prepare hot roll mix as directed on package, reducing water to ½ cup and adding sour cream and butter with egg. Cover; chill for about 45 minutes. Prepare frosting mix as directed on package.

Divide dough in half. Roll out each portion on well-floured surface to a 12x10-inch rectangle. Spread each with frosting; Sprinkle with nuts and coconut. Starting with 12-inch side, roll up jelly-roll fashion. Seal edges. Cut into 1-inch slices. Place, cut-side down, in greased muffin cups. Let rise in warm place until light, about 1 hour. Bake at 425° for 12 to 15 minutes until golden brown. Remove from pans immediately.

Tips: One half package (1½ cups firmly packed) two layer size frosting mix may be used. Prepare as directed on package, using half the butter and water.

If desired, use one can Pillsbury Ready-To-Spread Vanilla Frosting. Spread each 12x10-inch rectangle with ½ cup of frosting. Glaze warm rolls with remaining frosting.

MENU
Graduation Buffet Brunch
Fruit Kabobs
Broiled Ham Slices
Cheese Omelet
Nutty Buttercups
Double Butterscotch Crescents
Beverage

Butterscotch pudding mix in the dough plus butterscotch filling equals doubly rich crescents. In four hours you'll have these easy, delightful rolls you'll be proud to serve any time.

Double Butterscotch Crescents

    5 to 5½ cups Pillsbury's Best All Purpose Flour*
    2 teaspoons salt
    1 package active dry yeast
    1 package (4 oz.) butterscotch pudding and pie filling mix
    1½ cups milk
    ½ cup butter or margarine
    2 eggs

Filling

    ⅔ cup flaked coconut
    ⅔ cup firmly packed brown sugar
    ¼ cup butter or margarine, softened
    2 tablespoons flour
    ⅓ cup chopped pecans

OVEN 375°   36 ROLLS

In large mixer bowl, combine 2 cups of flour, salt and dry yeast. Prepare and cook pudding mix as directed on package, using 1½ cups milk. Remove from heat; add butter. Cool to lukewarm. Add pudding mixture and eggs to flour mixture. Blend at low speed until dry ingredients are moistened; beat 3 minutes at medium speed. By hand, stir in remaining flour to form a stiff dough. Cover; let rise in warm place until doubled in size, 1 to 1½ hours.

Prepare Filling. Divide dough into 3 portions. Roll out each portion on floured surface, to 15-inch circles. Cut each into 12 wedges. Place a rounded teaspoon of Filling on center of each wedge. Starting with wide end, roll up each toward point. Place, point-side down, on greased cookie sheets. Cover; let rise in warm place until doubled in size, about 1 hour. Bake at 375° for 12 to 15 minutes until golden brown. Drizzle with Vanilla Glaze, page 12 while warm.

Filling: In small mixer bowl, combine all ingredients except nuts. Blend at low speed for about 1 minute until well blended. Stir in nuts.

*For use with Pillsbury's Best Self-Rising Flour, omit salt.

Sweet enough for coffeetime spread with sweet and nutty icing. Or serve without icing and they're fancy enough for a black-tie dinner. Allow 1½ hours.

Sophie's Flaky French Crescents

   2½ to 3 cups Pillsbury's Best All Purpose
      Flour*
   2 tablespoons sugar
   1 teaspoon salt
   1 package active dry yeast
   1 cup milk
   ¼ cup shortening
   1 egg
   ½ cup butter or margarine, softened

Almond Icing
   1 cup confectioners' sugar
   ¼ cup chopped almonds
   1 tablespoon milk
   1 tablespoon butter or margarine, melted
   ½ teaspoon vanilla

OVEN 400°   20 ROLLS

In large mixer bowl, combine 1½ cups of flour, sugar, salt and dry yeast. In saucepan, heat milk and shortening until milk is warm. (Shortening does not need to melt.) Add egg and warm milk to dry ingredients. Blend at lowest speed until moistened; beat 3 minutes at medium speed. By hand, stir in remaining flour to form a stiff dough. Toss on floured surface until no longer sticky.

Roll out on floured surface to a square ¼-inch thick. Spread ⅔ of the dough with ⅓ of the butter. Fold unbuttered ⅓ of dough over ⅓ of buttered dough and the remaining ⅓ over all. Repeat rolling, spreading and folding process twice more, using ⅓ of the butter each time. Divide dough into 2 parts. Roll out each part on lightly floured surface to a 12-inch circle. Cut each circle into 10 wedges. Roll each wedge, starting with wide end and rolling to point. Place point-side down on greased cookie sheet, curving ends to form crescent. Cover; let rise in warm place until light and doubled in size, 45 to 60 minutes. Bake at 400° for 10 to 12 minutes until golden brown. For sweet rolls, frost with Almond Icing while warm.

Almond Icing: In small mixing bowl, combine all ingredients; mix well.

*Not recommended for use with Pillsbury's Best Self-Rising Flour.

A new twist on shape, and as good-tasting as they are pretty. Rich nut filling captured in an orange-flavored roll. Two hours a-making.

Ring-A-Lings

   4 to 4½ cups Pillsbury's Best All Purpose
      Flour*
   ⅓ cup sugar
   2 teaspoons salt
   2 packages active dry yeast
   2 teaspoons grated orange peel
   1 cup milk
   ⅓ cup butter or margarine
   2 eggs
   ¼ cup orange juice
   3 tablespoons sugar

Nut Filling
   ⅓ cup butter or margarine, softened
   1 cup confectioners' sugar
   1 cup finely chopped filberts or hazelnuts

OVEN 375°   22 ROLLS

In large mixer bowl, combine 2 cups of flour, sugar, salt, dry yeast and orange peel. In saucepan, heat milk and butter until milk is warm. (Butter does not need to melt.) Add eggs and warm milk to flour mixture. Blend at lowest speed until moistened; beat 3 minutes at medium speed. By hand, stir in remaining flour to form a stiff dough. Cover; let rest in warm place for 30 minutes.

Prepare Nut Filling. Roll out dough on floured surface to a 22x12-inch rectangle. Spread Filling over half of dough along 22-inch side. Fold uncovered dough over Filling. Cut crosswise into 1-inch strips. Twist each strip. Holding one end down on greased cookie sheet for center of roll, curl each strip around as for a pinwheel, tucking other end under. Cover; let rise in warm place until light and doubled in size, about 1 hour. Bake at 375° for 15 to 18 minutes until light golden brown. Combine orange juice and sugar. Brush on top of rolls. Remove from cookie sheets immediately.

Nut Filling: In small mixing bowl, combine butter and confectioners' sugar. Stir in nuts.

*For use with Pillsbury's Best Self-Rising Flour, omit salt.

Butterscotchy swirls — so pretty, so rich. Fun shape. Allow three hours, then serve warm.

Butter-Nut Swirls

3½ to 4 cups Pillsbury's Best All Purpose Flour*
⅓ cup instant nonfat dry milk
¼ cup sugar
1½ teaspoons salt
   1 package active dry yeast
   1 cup warm water
¼ cup butter, softened
   1 egg

<u>Filling</u>
½ cup butterscotch morsels
¼ cup firmly packed brown sugar
2 tablespoons honey
1 tablespoon butter
2 tablespoons flour
1 cup finely chopped walnuts

OVEN 375°   24 ROLLS

In large mixer bowl, combine 2 cups of flour, nonfat dry milk, sugar, salt and dry yeast. Add water, butter and egg. Blend at low speed until moistened; beat 3 minutes at medium speed. By hand, stir in remaining flour to form a stiff dough. Knead on floured surface until smooth and satiny, about 5 minutes. Place in greased bowl, turning to grease top. Cover; let rise in warm place until doubled in size, about 1½ hours. Prepare Filling.

Divide dough in half. Roll out each portion to a 14x12-inch rectangle. Spread Filling over half of each rectangle. Fold rectangles in half lengthwise, forming 12x7-inch rectangles. Pinch edges together. Cut each into 7x1-inch strips. Twist each strip and form circles, pinching ends, on cookie sheets, lined with well-greased aluminum foil. Cover; let rise in warm place until light and doubled in size, 30 to 45 minutes. Bake at 375° for 12 to 15 minutes until golden brown. Remove from pans immediately.

<u>Filling</u>: In small saucepan, melt all ingredients except flour and walnuts. Remove from heat; stir in flour and walnuts.

<u>Tips</u>: 1 cup milk may be used for dry milk and water; heat milk and butter until milk is warm.

Be creative with the shaping of rolls. After twisting the strips, make curlicues, strips or knots.

*For use with Pillsbury's Best Self-Rising Flour, omit salt.

88

Quick, easy rolls made with hot roll mix for all the peanut butter lovers. Peanut butter and honey glaze creates a yummy, moist roll . . . in a little over an hour.

Peanut Glazed Rolls

I package Pillsbury Hot Roll Mix

Topping and Filling
- ½ cup sugar
- ¼ cup butter or margarine
- ¼ cup cream or evaporated milk
- 2 tablespoons peanut butter
- 2 tablespoons honey
- ½ cup salted peanuts, chopped

OVEN 350°   16 ROLLS

Prepare hot roll mix as directed on package. Prepare Topping. After first rise, roll out dough on floured surface to a 12x8-inch rectangle. Spread with half of Topping and Filling. Roll up dough, jelly-roll fashion, starting with 12-inch side. Seal edges. Cut into 16 slices. Place cut-side down in two well-greased 8-inch round layer pans. Cover; let rise in warm place until light and doubled in size, about 30 minutes. Bake at 350° for 20 to 25 minutes until golden brown. Cool about 5 minutes; invert onto serving plate. Spread with remaining Topping. Serve warm.

Topping and Filling: In small mixer bowl, combine all ingredients except peanuts: beat at low speed until smooth. Stir in peanuts.

89

No-knead, rich with egg, yeast rolls. Orange syrup gives an excellent base to this yummy roll. Dough can be refrigerated, too, and baked up to 3 days later.

Orange Glory Rolls

Rolls
 7½ to 8 cups Pillsbury's Best All Purpose
    Flour*
 ½ cup sugar
 2 teaspoons salt
 2 packages active dry yeast
 2 cups warm water
 ¼ cup shortening
 2 eggs
    Melted butter

Orange Sauce
 1½ cups sugar
 6 tablespoons butter or margarine
 3 tablespoons grated orange peel
 ¾ cup orange juice

OVEN 375°   36 ROLLS

Rolls: In large mixer bowl, combine 2 cups of flour, sugar, salt and dry yeast; add water, shortening and eggs. Blend at lowest speed until moistened; beat 3 minutes at medium speed. By hand, stir in remaining flour to form a stiff dough. Toss on floured surface until no longer sticky. Let rest while preparing Orange Sauce.

Divide dough into 3 portions. Roll out each portion to a 12x10-inch rectangle. Brush with melted butter. Roll up each, starting with 12-inch edge. Cut into 1-inch slices. Place, cut-side down, on Orange Sauce in greased muffin cups. Let rise in warm place until light and doubled in size, 45 to 60 minutes. Bake at 375° for 15 to 20 minutes until golden brown. Let stand 30 seconds; invert onto serving plate allowing sauce to glaze rolls.

Orange Sauce: In saucepan, combine all ingredients. Bring to boil over medium heat; simmer for 5 minutes, stirring occasionally. Divide mixture into well-greased muffin cups. Place a scant tablespoon of mixture in each of 36 medium muffin cups.

Tips: For a quick Orange Sauce, heat 2 cups orange marmalade with 6 tablespoons butter or margarine.

If you don't have 36 muffin cups, you may refrigerate dough and Orange Sauce up to three days. Reheat sauce before using.

If desired, bake 18 rolls in muffin cups and the remaining 18 rolls in two 8 or 9-inch round layer pans. Use about ½ cup sauce in each greased pan and bake 20 to 25 minutes.

*For use with Pillsbury's Best Self-Rising Flour, omit salt.

Twist wild and wonderful shapes from brown-sugared strips of dough. Make dough early and chill. Shape and bake in an hour and a quarter.

Almond Rolls

 3¼ cups Pillsbury's Best All Purpose Flour*
 1 tablespoon sugar
 1 teaspoon salt
 1 package active dry yeast
 ½ cup butter or margarine
 ¼ cup shortening
 2 eggs, beaten
 ⅔ cup dairy sour cream
 ¼ cup warm water
 1 teaspoon almond extract
 ⅔ cup firmly packed brown sugar
 ½ cup chopped almonds

OVEN 350°   ABOUT 36 ROLLS

In large mixing bowl, combine flour, sugar, salt and dry yeast. Cut in butter and shortening until particles are the size of small peas. Add eggs, sour cream, warm water and almond extract; mix well. Cover; chill at least 2 hours or overnight.

Punch down dough. Sprinkle brown sugar on floured surface. Roll out dough in sugar with rolling pin, folding over and re-rolling until all sugar is used and dough is about ¼-inch thick. Sprinkle with almonds, pressing in with rolling pin. Cut dough into 6x1-inch strips. Twist strips and form into sticks, circles or "S" shapes. Place on greased cookie sheets. Cover; let rise in warm place until light and doubled in size, 45 to 60 minutes. Bake at 350° for 15 to 20 minutes until golden brown. If desired, drizzle with Almond Glaze, page 12, while warm.

*For use with Pillsbury's Best Self-Rising Flour, omit salt.

Lemon, nutmeg and mace team to make sugary special tea rolls, ready in about 3 hours.

Lucky Lemon Clovers

    5 to 5½ cups Pillsbury's Best All Purpose
        Flour*
    ½ cup sugar
    2 teaspoons salt
    ½ teaspoon nutmeg
    ½ teaspoon cinnamon
    ¼ teaspoon mace
    2 packages active dry yeast
    1¼ cups milk
    ½ cup shortening
    2 eggs
    1 teaspoon lemon extract
    1 cup sugar
    ½ teaspoon nutmeg
    1 tablespoon grated lemon peel
    ¼ cup butter or margarine, melted

OVEN 375°   24 ROLLS

In large mixer bowl, combine 2 cups of flour, sugar, salt, spices and dry yeast. In saucepan, heat milk and shortening until milk is warm. (Shortening does not need to melt.) Add eggs, lemon extract and warm milk to flour mixture. Blend at lowest speed until moistened; beat 3 minutes at medium speed. By hand, stir in remaining flour to form a stiff dough. Knead on floured surface until smooth and elastic, about 3 minutes. Place in greased bowl, turning to grease top. Cover; let rise in warm place until light and doubled in size, 1 to 1½ hours. In small mixing bowl, combine sugar, nutmeg and lemon peel. Set aside.

Punch down dough; divide in half. Shape each portion into 12 round balls. Dip each in melted butter, then in sugar mixture. Place in well-greased muffin cups. With scissors, cut rolls in half, then in quarters, almost to bottom of roll to form a cloverleaf. Cover; let rise in warm place until light and doubled in size, 30 to 45 minutes. Bake at 375° for 15 to 20 minutes until golden brown. Remove from muffin cups immediately.

*For use with Pillsbury's Best Self-Rising Flour, omit salt.

Cinnamon-coiled rolls that are very light and tender, topped with brown-sugary pineapple. Allow three hours in all.

Pineapple Supreme Rolls

    4½ to 4¾ cups Pillsbury's Best All Purpose
        Flour*
    ¼ cup sugar
    2 teaspoons salt
    1 package active dry yeast
    1¼ cups milk
    2 tablespoons shortening
    1 egg
    2 tablespoons butter or margarine, melted
    ⅓ cup sugar
    2 teaspoons cinnamon

Pineapple Topping
    ¼ cup butter or margarine
    ⅔ cup firmly packed brown sugar
    1 can (13¼ oz.) crushed pineapple, drained

OVEN 375°   15 ROLLS

In large mixer bowl, combine 2 cups of flour, sugar, salt and dry yeast. In saucepan, heat milk and shortening until milk is warm. (Shortening does not need to melt.) Add egg and warm milk to flour mixture. Blend at lowest speed until moistened; beat 3 minutes at medium speed. By hand, stir in remaining flour to form a stiff dough. Knead on floured surface until smooth and elastic, about 3 minutes. Place in greased bowl, turning to grease top. Cover; let rise in warm place until light and doubled in size, 1 to 1½ hours. Prepare Pineapple Topping.

Punch down dough. Roll out on floured surface to a 15x12-inch rectangle. Brush with 2 tablespoons melted butter; sprinkle with mixture of sugar and cinnamon. Roll up, starting with 15-inch side. Cut into 1-inch slices. Place cut-side down over Pineapple Topping in 13x9-inch pan. Cover; let rise in warm place until light and doubled in size, 45 to 60 minutes. Bake at 375° for 20 to 25 minutes until golden brown. Loosen sides and turn out immediately.

Pineapple Topping: In 13x9-inch pan, melt butter. Add brown sugar and pineapple; stir to blend.

*For use with Pillsbury's Best Self-Rising Flour, omit salt.

Butter-layered crescents hide the secret of a butter-coconut filling — a treasure indeed. Allow three hours, or only 30 minutes with quick tip.

Coconut Butter Pastries

4½ to 5 cups Pillsbury's Best All Purpose Flour*
⅓ cup sugar
1½ teaspoons salt
¼ teaspoon nutmeg
1 teaspoon grated orange peel
1 package active dry yeast
1 ¼ cups milk
¼ cup butter or margarine
2 eggs (reserve one yolk)
½ teaspoon vanilla
¼ cup butter or margarine, softened

Filling
½ cup sugar
3 tablespoons butter or margarine, softened
1 cup flaked coconut
Reserved egg yolk

OVEN 400°   24 ROLLS

In large mixer bowl, combine 2 cups of flour, sugar, salt, nutmeg, orange peel and dry yeast. In saucepan, heat milk and ¼ cup butter until milk is warm. (Butter does not need to melt.) Add warm milk, eggs and vanilla to dry ingredients. Mix at low speed until moistened; beat 3 minutes at medium speed. By hand, stir in remaining flour. Cover; let rise in warm place until light and doubled in size, about 1½ hours.

Punch down dough; roll out on floured surface to a 14-inch square. Spread half of dough with half of butter to within 2 inches of edges. Fold dough in half and then in quarters; seal edges. Repeat process, using remaining butter. Cover; let rest 15 minutes. Prepare Filling.

Divide dough in thirds. Roll out each third on floured surface to a 9-inch circle. Cut each circle into 8 wedges. Place a scant teaspoon of Filling in center of each wedge and roll up starting from widest end. Place, point-side down, on ungreased cookie sheets. Cover; let rise in warm place until light and doubled in size, about 30 minutes. Bake at 400° for 10 to 12 minutes until golden brown. If desired, drizzle with Vanilla Glaze, page 12.

Filling: Blend sugar with butter. Add coconut and egg yolk; mix well.

Tip: For quick Coconut Butter Pastries, use 1 package Pillsbury Refrigerated Quick Crescent Dinner Rolls. Prepare Filling, using ¼ cup sugar, 1½ tablespoons butter, ½ cup flaked coconut and 1 egg yolk. Place a scant tablespoon of Filling in center of each triangle before rolling up. Bake as directed **above**.

*For use with Pillsbury's Best Self-Rising Flour, omit salt.

Pineapple stars beautifully in this cinnamon roll variation. Grated orange peel adds tang, too, in this 2½ hour sweet roll.

Cinnamon Pine-Rolls

4 to 4½ cups Pillsbury's Best All Purpose Flour*
¼ cup sugar
2 teaspoons salt
2 packages active dry yeast
I cup milk
½ cup shortening
2 eggs
2 teaspoons grated orange peel
¼ cup butter or margarine, melted
I can (I lb. 4 oz.) crushed pineapple, drain and reserve 2 tablespoons pineapple and 2 tablespoons syrup
½ cup firmly packed brown sugar
I teaspoon cinnamon

Topping

½ cup firmly packed brown sugar
2 tablespoons reserved crushed pineapple
2 tablespoons reserved pineapple syrup
2 tablespoons butter or margarine, melted

OVEN 375°   24 ROLLS

In large mixer bowl, combine 2 cups of flour, sugar, salt and dry yeast. In saucepan, heat milk and shortening until milk is warm. (Shortening does not need to melt.) Add eggs, orange peel and warm milk to flour mixture. Blend at lowest speed until moistened; beat 3 minutes at medium speed. By hand, stir in remaining flour to form a stiff dough. Knead on floured surface until smooth and elastic, about 3 minutes. Place in greased bowl, turning to grease top. Cover; let rise in warm place until light and doubled in size, I to I½ hours.

Punch down dough; divide in half. Roll out one half on floured surface to a 12x10-inch rectangle. Brush with half the melted butter. Spread on ½ cup of the drained crushed pineapple. Combine brown sugar and cinnamon; sprinkle half over pineapple. Roll up starting with 12-inch side; seal edges. Cut into I-inch slices. Place, cut-side down, in well-greased 9-inch round layer pan. Repeat with remaining dough. Cover; let rise in warm place until light and doubled in size, 30 to 45 minutes. Bake at 375° for 20 to 25 minutes until golden brown. Brush on Topping. Return to oven and bake 5

minutes more. Remove from pans immediately.

Topping: In small mixing bowl, combine brown sugar, crushed pineapple, pineapple syrup and melted butter. Mix well.

*For use with Pillsbury's Best Self-Rising Flour, omit salt.

Sweet rolls with a hint of lemon in the dough and swirled with lemon sugar. Potato in the dough makes them light and tender. Prepare in about two and a half hours.

Lemon Nut Rolls

I package Pillsbury Hot Roll Mix
⅓ cup Pillsbury Hungry Jack Mashed Potato Flakes
I tablespoon grated lemon peel
2 tablespoons butter or margarine, melted
¾ cup sugar
½ cup chopped pecans
2 teaspoons grated lemon peel

OVEN 375°   16 ROLLS

Prepare hot roll mix as directed on package, adding dry potato flakes and I tablespoon lemon peel to the softened yeast. After first rise, toss dough on floured surface until no longer sticky. Roll out to a 16x12-inch rectangle. Brush with melted butter. In small mixing bowl, combine sugar, pecans and lemon peel. Sprinkle mixture over dough. Roll up starting with 16-inch side; seal edges. Cut into I-inch slices. Place, cut-side down, in two well-greased 8 or 9-inch round layer pans. Cover; let rise in warm place until light and doubled in size, 30 to 45 minutes. Bake at 375° for 20 to 25 minutes until golden brown. Remove from pans immediately.

How simple with hot roll mix, coconut-almond frosting mix and apricot preserves! Rich and chewy . . . serve them warm. Allow yourself an hour and a half.

Apricot Dandies

    1 package Pillsbury Hot Roll Mix
 ¾ cup apricot preserves
    Reserved ½ cup frosting mix

Topping
 ⅓ cup butter or margarine, melted
 ¼ cup orange juice
    3 tablespoons firmly packed brown sugar
    1 package Pillsbury Coconut-Almond
    Frosting Mix (reserve ½ cup)

OVEN 375°   15 ROLLS

Prepare hot roll mix as directed on package. Prepare Topping. After first rise, toss dough on well-floured surface until no longer sticky. Roll out to a 15x12-inch rectangle. Spread with apricot preserves and sprinkle with reserved ½ cup of frosting mix. Starting with 15-inch side, roll up jelly-roll fashion. Seal edges. Cut into 1-inch slices. Place, cut-side down, in prepared pan. Cover; let rise until light and doubled in size, about 30 minutes. Bake at 375° for 25 to 30 minutes, until golden brown. Invert *immediately* onto cooling rack. Serve warm.

Topping: Melt butter in 13x9-inch pan. Stir in orange juice and brown sugar; blend well. Sprinkle with frosting mix; stir until moistened. Spread evenly over bottom of pan.

Tip: Substitute pineapple preserves for apricot preserves to make "pineapple dandies".

A pretty shape to any roll. Try the tip for quick "Posies" for your next coffee party. Hot roll mix or refrigerated biscuits — they're both easy and pretty.

Sweet Posies

    1 package Pillsbury Hot Roll Mix
    2 teaspoons vanilla
    3 tablespoons butter or margarine, melted
 ⅓ cup sugar
    1 teaspoon cinnamon
    Cake and pastry filling or prepared
    pie filling
    Chopped nuts, if desired

OVEN 375°   ABOUT 18 ROLLS

Prepare hot roll mix as directed on package, adding vanilla with egg. After first rise, toss dough on well-floured surface until no longer sticky. Roll out to ¼-inch thickness. Cut into rounds with 3-inch cutter. Dip tops in melted butter; then in mixture of sugar and cinnamon. Place rounds, 1 inch apart, on greased cookie sheets. Place point of scissors in middle of roll; clip through roll from outside to center to make 7 petals. Do not separate petals. Cover; let rise in warm place until light and doubled in size, about 1 hour. Place a rounded teaspoon of favorite cake and pastry filling or pie filling in center of each roll. Bake at 375° for 12 to 15 minutes until golden brown. Sprinkle center with nuts. If desired drizzle petals with Vanilla Glaze, page 12. Serve warm.

Tip: For quick "Posies", use Pillsbury Refrigerated Biscuits. Dip in butter and cinnamon-sugar as directed. Bake at 375° for 10 to 12 minutes. Place a teaspoonful of jam or a maraschino cherry in center of roll after baking.

(Sweet Posies)
Place point of scissors in middle of roll; clip through roll from outside to center to make 7 petals.

Cinnamon rolls gone mad with mincemeat and apple cider. Even a cider glaze. Easy no-knead yeast dough prepared in about three hours.

Cinnamince Cider Buns

3½ to 4 cups Pillsbury's Best All Purpose Flour*
  3 tablespoons sugar
1½ teaspoons salt
  I package active dry yeast
  I cup warm water
¼ cup shortening
  I egg
¼ cup firmly packed brown sugar
1½ teaspoons cinnamon
  2 tablespoons butter or margarine

Mincemeat Filling
½ cup (½ of 9 oz. package) dry mincemeat
½ cup apple cider

Cider Glaze
¾ cup confectioners' sugar
¾ teaspoon cinnamon
1½ tablespoons apple cider

OVEN 350°   TWO 8-INCH COFFEE CAKES

In large mixing bowl, combine 2 cups of flour, sugar, salt and dry yeast. Add warm water, shortening and egg. Beat until smooth. Stir in remaining flour to form a stiff dough. Place in greased bowl, turning to grease top. Cover; let rise in warm place until light and doubled in size, I to 1½ hours. Prepare Filling.

Punch down dough. Roll out on floured surface to a 26x9-inch rectangle. Spread on Mincemeat Filling. Combine brown sugar and cinnamon; sprinkle over filling. Dot with butter. Roll up starting with 26-inch edge. Cut into 1½-inch slices. Place cut-side down in two well-greased 8-inch round layer pans. Cover; let rise in warm place until doubled in size, 45 to 60 minutes. Bake at 350° for 30 to 35 minutes until golden brown. Remove from pans immediately. While warm, drizzle with Cider Glaze.

Mincemeat Filling: In saucepan, combine dry mincemeat and apple cider. Break up mincemeat slightly with spoon. Bring to a boil; boil vigorously for I minute, stirring constantly. Cool.

Cider Glaze: In small mixing bowl, combine confectioners' sugar, cinnamon and apple cider; mix well.

*For use with Pillsbury's Best Self-Rising Flour, omit salt.

Sweet raisins peek through orange fan tans, topped with sugary-nut goodness. Hot roll mix makes them extra quick and easy.

Fan-Tasties

  I package Pillsbury Hot Roll Mix
  I tablespoon grated orange peel
  I cup raisins or currants
  2 tablespoons butter or margarine, melted
  2 tablespoons firmly packed brown sugar
  2 tablespoons confectioners' sugar
  I teaspoon grated orange peel
⅓ cup finely chopped nuts

OVEN 375°   18 ROLLS

Prepare hot roll mix as directed on package, adding orange peel and raisins with flour mixture. Cover; let rise in warm place until light and doubled in size, 30 to 45 minutes.

Punch down dough; roll out on well-floured surface to a 14x10-inch rectangle. Brush with melted butter. Combine brown sugar, confectioners' sugar, grated orange peel and chopped nuts; sprinkle over dough. Cut into 8 long strips. Stack 4 strips together. Cut stacks into 9 pieces each and place cut-side down in well-greased muffin cups. Cover; let rise in warm place until light and doubled in size, about 30 minutes. Bake at 375° for 15 to 20 minutes until golden brown.

Sunny-Side-Up Rolls

3¾ to 4 cups Pillsbury's Best All Purpose
    Flour*
⅓ cup sugar
2 teaspoons salt
2 packages active dry yeast
1 cup milk
⅓ cup butter or margarine
1 egg
⅓ cup sugar
1 teaspoon cinnamon
1 tablespoon butter or margarine, melted

Topping
½ cup firmly packed brown sugar
½ cup dairy sour cream
¼ cup sugar
15 drained, unpeeled apricot halves
    (1 lb. 14 oz. can)

OVEN 375°   15 ROLLS

In large mixer bowl, combine 2 cups of flour, sugar, salt and dry yeast. In saucepan, heat milk and butter until milk is warm. (Butter does not need to melt.) Add warm milk and egg to flour mixture. Blend at low speed until moistened; beat 3 minutes at medium speed. By hand, stir in remaining flour to form a stiff dough. Cover; let rise in warm place until light and doubled in size, about 30 minutes. Prepare Topping. Combine sugar and cinnamon.

Punch down dough; roll out on floured surface to a 15x9-inch rectangle. Brush with melted butter; sprinkle with cinnamon-sugar mixture. Roll up starting with 15-inch side. Seal edges. Cut into 1-inch slices. Place each roll on an apricot half in prepared pan. Cover; let rise in warm place until light, about 1 hour. Bake at 375° for 20 to 25 minutes until deep golden brown. Invert immediately onto wire rack or serving plate; let stand 2 to 3 minutes before removing pan.

Topping: In saucepan, combine brown sugar, sour cream, and sugar. Bring to a boil; boil 3 minutes. Spread in a well-greased 13x9-inch pan. Arrange apricots, cut-side down, over sour cream mixture.

*For use with Pillsbury's Best Self-Rising Flour, omit salt.

Blind Date Surprise Rolls

3¾ to 4¼ cups Pillsbury's Best All Purpose
    Flour*
¼ cup sugar
1½ teaspoons salt
2 packages active dry yeast
½ cup milk
¼ cup butter or margarine
¾ cup dairy sour cream
1 egg

Date Filling
2 tablespoons butter or margarine
⅓ cup firmly packed brown sugar
½ teaspoon cinnamon
⅛ teaspoon nutmeg
1 cup chopped dates
¼ cup chopped nuts

OVEN 350°   18 ROLLS

In large mixing bowl, combine 1½ cups of flour, sugar, salt and dry yeast. In saucepan, heat milk and butter until milk is warm. (Butter does not need to melt.) Add sour cream, egg and warm milk to flour mixture. Stir to combine; beat until smooth. Stir in remaining flour to form a stiff dough. Toss on floured surface until no longer sticky. Cover; let rest while preparing Date Filling. Divide dough into 20 pieces. Shape each into a ball. Make indentation on bottom of roll. Place one tablespoon of Date Filling in each roll. Seal filling inside dough by pinching edges together. Place seam-side down on greased cookie sheets. Cover; let rise in warm place until light and doubled in size, about 1 hour. Bake at 350° for 15 to 18 minutes until golden brown. Frost with Vanilla Frosting, page 12. Serve warm or cold.

Date Filling: In saucepan, melt butter. Stir in remaining ingredients.

*For use with Pillsbury's Best Self-Rising Flour, omit salt.

A rich and flaky crisp roll, layered with orange and sprinkled with sugared pecans. A Danish delight, prepared in about four hours.

Orange Danish Krispies

    5 to 5½ cups Pillsbury's Best All Purpose
        Flour*
    ½ cup sugar
    2 teaspoons salt
    I package active dry yeast
    1¼ cups milk
    ½ cup butter or margarine
    3 eggs, reserve I egg white for glaze
    4 tablespoons grated orange peel
    ¾ cup sugar
    ½ cup butter or margarine, melted
    ⅓ cup orange juice
    I cup chopped pecans
    ⅓ cup sugar

OVEN 400°   24 KRISPIES

In large mixer bowl, combine 2 cups of flour, sugar, salt and dry yeast. In saucepan, heat milk and butter until milk is warm. (Butter does not need to melt.) Add 2 eggs and I egg yolk, 2 tablespoons orange peel and warm milk to flour mixture. Blend at low speed until moistened; beat 3 minutes at medium speed. By hand, stir in remaining flour to form a stiff dough. Cover; let rise in warm place until light and doubled in size, 1½ to 2 hours.

Line 4 cookie sheets (see Tip) with aluminum foil and grease well. Turn up edges to form a rim. In small mixing bowl, combine ¾ cup sugar and 2 tablespoons orange peel; set aside. Stir down dough; toss on well-floured surface until no longer sticky. Roll out on well-floured surface to a 20x10-inch rectangle. Brush with 2 tablespoons of the melted butter; sprinkle with ¼ cup of orange-sugar mixture. Fold dough in thirds. Turn dough ¼ way around. Repeat process 2 more times. Roll dough again to a 20x10-inch rectangle. Brush with remaining melted butter. Cut in half to make two 10-inch squares. Roll up each, starting with 10-inch edge. Cut each roll into 12 slices. Place slices 3 inches apart on greased foil-lined cookie sheets. With fingers, flatten rolls to ¼-inch thickness. Combine orange juice and reserved egg white; brush rolls, using all of mixture. Combine pecans and sugar; sprinkle over rolls,

pressing pecans into rolls. Let rise in warm place until light and doubled in size, 30 to 45 minutes. Bake at 400° for I2 to I5 minutes until light golden brown. Remove from sheets immediately.

Tip: If necessary, place slices on greased foil and then transfer foil to cookie sheets as pans are available for baking.

*For use with Pillsbury's Best Self-Rising Flour, omit salt.

It looks like a bear claw; tastes like a doughnut. Serve them warm and sugary in 2½ hours. Yum!

Doughboys

    6 to 6½ cups Pillsbury's Best All Purpose
        Flour*
    ½ cup sugar
    2 teaspoons salt
    I package active dry yeast
    2⅓ cups milk
    ⅓ cup shortening
    ½ to I teaspoon anise seed, if desired
    I egg

DEEP FAT 375°   30 DOUGHBOYS

In large mixer bowl, combine 2 cups of flour, sugar, salt and dry yeast. In saucepan, heat milk and shortening until milk is warm. (Shortening does not need to melt.) Add anise seed, egg and warm milk to flour mixture. Blend at lowest speed until moistened. Beat 2 minutes at medium speed. By hand, stir in remaining flour to form a stiff dough. Cover; let rise in warm place until light and doubled in size, about I hour.

Divide dough in half. Roll out each half on floured surface to a I2x10-inch rectangle. Cut into 4x2-inch strips. Cut about half-way across each strip at two intervals on 4-inch side. Cover; let rise in warm place until light and doubled in size, about 45 minutes. Fry in deep, hot fat (375°) I to 2 minutes on each side, until golden brown. Drain. Roll in sugar, if desired.

Tip: Instead of deep-fat frying the doughboys, fry in frypan with ⅛-inch melted butter over medium heat for about 2 minutes on each side. Roll in sugar while warm.

*For use with Pillsbury's Best Self-Rising Flour, omit salt.

They'll flip when you tell them what's in these light golden sticky buns: sweet potatoes! Very yellow, mellow and good. Two and a half hours.

Yam-Yam Honey Buns

3¼ to 3¾ cups Pillsbury's Best All Purpose Flour*
¼ cup sugar
2 teaspoons salt
2 packages active dry yeast
½ cup mashed sweet potatoes or yams
2 tablespoons butter or margarine, softened
1 teaspoon vanilla
½ cup warm water
2 eggs
2 tablespoons butter or margarine, melted
¼ cup firmly packed brown sugar
½ cup chopped nuts

Topping
¼ cup butter or margarine
½ cup firmly packed brown sugar
⅓ cup honey
¼ teaspoon salt

OVEN 375°   18 ROLLS

In large mixing bowl, combine 2 cups of flour, sugar, salt and dry yeast. Stir in sweet potatoes, butter, vanilla, water and eggs. Beat until smooth. Stir in remaining flour to form a stiff dough. Cover; let rise in warm place until light and doubled in size, 1 to 1½ hours.

Prepare Topping. Stir down dough. Toss on floured surface until no longer sticky. Roll out to an 18x10-inch rectangle. Spread with melted butter; sprinkle with brown sugar and nuts. Roll up jelly-roll fashion, starting with 18-inch side. Cut into 1-inch slices. Place cut-side down in prepared pan. Cover; let rise in warm place until light and doubled in size, about 45 minutes. Bake at 375° for 30 to 35 minutes until golden brown. Invert immediately onto serving plate or cooling rack.

Topping: Melt butter in bottom of 13x9-inch pan. Stir in remaining ingredients; spread to cover bottom of pan.

Tip: Rolls may be made in two 9-inch round layer pans. Bake for 25 to 30 minutes.

*For use with Pillsbury's Best Self-Rising Flour, omit salt.

Crispy rolls studded with raisins and spiced with cinnamon and brown sugar. A snap to make in 1¾ hours. Note the tip for refrigerated dough.

Cinnamon Nut Crisps

2 to 2½ cups Pillsbury's Best All Purpose Flour*
1 tablespoon sugar
½ teaspoon salt
1 package active dry yeast
¾ cup warm water
2 tablespoons butter or margarine, softened
½ teaspoon vanilla
1 egg
2 tablespoons butter or margarine, melted
½ cup firmly packed brown sugar
½ teaspoon cinnamon
¼ cup raisins
¼ cup chopped nuts

OVEN 375°   16 ROLLS

In large mixer bowl, combine 1 cup of flour, sugar, salt and dry yeast. Add warm water, butter, vanilla and egg. Blend at lowest speed until moistened; beat 3 minutes at medium speed. By hand, stir in remaining flour to form a stiff dough. Cover; let rise in warm place until light and doubled in size, about 1 hour.

Toss on well-floured surface until no longer sticky. Roll out dough on floured surface to a 16x10-inch rectangle. Spread with melted butter; sprinkle with brown sugar, cinnamon, raisins and nuts. Starting with 16-inch side, roll up jelly-roll fashion. Seal edges. Cut into sixteen 1-inch slices. Place cut-side down on greased cookie sheets, 2 inches apart. With fingers, flatten each slice to ⅛-inch thickness. Sprinkle each with additional sugar and cinnamon. Bake at 375° for 18 to 20 minutes until golden brown. Serve warm.

Tips: Pillsbury Hot Roll Mix makes delicious Cinnamon Nut Crisps. Prepare as directed on package, adding ½ teaspoon vanilla. Shape and bake as directed above.

For really quick Nut Crisps, use 1 package Pillsbury Refrigerated Quick Danish Cinnamon Rolls with Icing. Place cut-side down on greased cookie sheets. Flatten. Sprinkle with chopped nuts and cinnamon-sugar. Bake at 375° for 10 to 12 minutes until golden brown. Thin icing if necessary; then drizzle over rolls.

*For use with Pillsbury's Best Self-Rising Flour, omit salt.

Dark and textury English muffins, with the nutty bite of rolled oats and the homey flavor of molasses. An easy, make-ahead breakfast treat.

English Oatwheels

    4 to 4½ cups Pillsbury's Best All Purpose
        Flour*
    1 cup quick-cooking rolled oats
    2 tablespoons firmly packed brown sugar
    1 teaspoon salt
    1 package active dry yeast
    1¼ cups warm water
    ¼ cup cooking oil
    1 egg
    2 tablespoons molasses
        Cornmeal

GRIDDLE 300°   18 ENGLISH MUFFINS

In large mixer bowl, combine 2 cups of flour, rolled oats, brown sugar, salt and dry yeast. Add warm water, oil, egg and molasses. Blend at lowest speed until moistened; beat 3 minutes at medium speed. By hand, stir in remaining flour to form a stiff dough. Cover; let rest in warm place for 30 minutes.

Toss dough on floured surface until no longer sticky. Roll out to ⅜-inch thickness. Cut with 3-inch round cutter. Place on greased cookie sheet, sprinkled with cornmeal. Cover; let rise in warm place until light and doubled in size, 30 to 45 minutes. Bake slowly on moderately hot griddle (300°), about 7 minutes on each side, until brown. Split cooled muffins, toast cut sides up; serve with butter and jam or jelly.

*For use with Pillsbury's Best Self-Rising Flour, omit salt.

(Cinnamon Nut Crisps) With fingers, flatten each slice.

Thin rounds of rich, flaky layers, rerolled three times with cinnamon-sugar. A delight to serve with coffee. Ready in about three hours.

Butter Crispies

    6 to 6½ cups Pillsbury's Best All Purpose
        Flour*
    ½ cup sugar
    1¼ teaspoons salt
    1 package active dry yeast
    1½ cups milk
    ½ cup shortening
    2 eggs
    1 teaspoon lemon extract
    6 tablespoons butter or margarine, softened
    ¾ cup sugar
    4 teaspoons cinnamon
    ¾ cup sugar

OVEN 400°   30 CRISPIES

In large mixer bowl, combine 2 cups of flour, sugar, salt and dry yeast. In saucepan, heat milk and shortening until milk is warm. (Shortening does not need to melt.) Add eggs, lemon extract and warm milk to flour mixture. Blend at lowest speed until moistened; beat 3 minutes at medium speed. By hand, stir in remaining flour to form a stiff dough. Knead on floured surface until smooth and elastic, about 5 minutes. Place in greased bowl, turning to grease top. Cover; let rise in warm place until light and doubled in size, 1 to 1½ hours.

Punch down dough; roll out on floured surface to a 15x12-inch rectangle. Spread half of dough with 2 tablespoons butter; sprinkle on ¼ cup of the sugar. Fold unbuttered side over buttered side; seal edges. Roll out again to a 15x12-inch rectangle. Repeating butter and sugar measurements, spread and roll dough two more times, ending with 15x12-inch rectangle.

Combine cinnamon and sugar; sprinkle half over the dough. Roll up, starting with 15-inch side. Cut into ½-inch slices. Place on well-greased cookie sheets and flatten to about ¼-inch thickness with palm of hand. Sprinkle with remaining cinnamon-sugar mixture. Let rise in warm place, 15 to 20 minutes. Bake at 400° for 10 to 12 minutes. Remove from baking sheets immediately. Store in tightly covered container.

*For use with Pillsbury's Best Self-Rising Flour, omit salt.

Raised doughnuts swirled with cinnamon 'n sugar and glazed — ready in zig-time.

Cinnamon Whirl Doughnuts

   6 to 7 cups Pillsbury's Best All Purpose
     Flour*
 ½ cup sugar
 3 teaspoons salt
 2 packages active dry yeast
 2 cups milk
 ¼ cup butter or margarine
  I egg
 3½ teaspoons cinnamon
 2 tablespoons sugar

DEEP FAT 375°   36 DOUGHNUTS

In large mixer bowl, combine 3 cups of flour, sugar, salt and dry yeast. In saucepan, heat milk and butter until milk is warm. (Butter does not need to melt.) Add egg and warm milk to flour mixture. Blend at lowest speed until moistened; beat 3 minutes at medium speed. By hand, stir in remaining flour to form a stiff dough. Knead on floured surface until smooth and elastic, about 3 minutes. Place in greased bowl, turning to grease top. Cover; let rise in warm place until light and doubled in size, I to I½ hours.

Punch down dough; divide in half. Roll out each portion on floured surface to an 18x8-inch rectangle. Sprinkle each with cinnamon-sugar mixture to within I inch of edge. Roll up jelly-roll fashion starting with 18-inch edge. Seal edges well. Cut into ½-inch slices. Place on ungreased cookie sheets. Do not cover; let rise in warm place until light and doubled in size, 30 to 45 minutes. Fry in deep hot fat (375°), I½ to 2 minutes on each side. Drain on absorbent paper. While warm, dip tops in Vanilla Glaze, page 12.

*For use with Pillsbury's Best Self-Rising Flour, omit salt.

MENU
"Hobgoblin" Party
Apples
Popcorn Balls
Coffee-Time Doughnuts
Cinnamon Whirl Doughnuts
Hot Chocolate

Put your own topping on these light, raised doughnuts. Just 3 hours from start to finish, then sugar or glaze . . . they're sure to be a hit.

Coffee-Time Doughnuts

 3½ to 3¾ cups Pillsbury's Best All Purpose
     Flour*
 ¼ cup sugar
 I½ teaspoons salt
  I teaspoon nutmeg
  I package active dry yeast
  I cup milk
 ¼ cup shortening
  I egg

DEEP FAT 375°   24 DOUGHNUTS

In large mixing bowl, combine I cup of flour, sugar, salt, nutmeg and dry yeast. In saucepan, heat milk and shortening until milk is warm. (Shortening does not need to melt.) Add egg and warm milk to flour mixture. Beat until smooth. Stir in remaining flour to form a stiff dough. Cover; let rise in warm place until light and doubled in size, about I hour.

Punch down dough. Roll out on floured surface to ½-inch thickness. Cut with 3½-inch floured doughnut cutter. Cover; let rise in warm place until light and doubled in size, about 30 to 45 minutes. Fry in deep hot fat (375°) about 2 minutes on each side until golden brown. Drain on absorbent paper. While warm, roll in sugar, or dip in Vanilla Glaze, page 12.

*For use with Pillsbury's Best Self-Rising Flour, omit salt.

Quick Breads

● When you haven't the time to make yeast bread, here's a galaxy of smart quick breads that can step in and play a starring role in your brunch, lunch or dinner. Half the fun of quick bread is the variety from which you can choose: muffins, biscuits, coffee cakes, doughnuts, nut bread or attractive steamed breads. Make them easy; then serve them warm or cold.

Blueberry muffin mixture masquerades as a nut bread, and surprises your palate with a hint of orange. Make it early for ease in slicing.

Blueberry Brunch Loaf

2¼ cups Pillsbury's Best All Purpose Flour*
¾ cup firmly packed brown sugar
3 teaspoons baking powder
1 teaspoon salt
¼ cup butter or margarine, softened
1 egg
1 tablespoon grated orange peel
½ cup milk
¼ cup orange juice
1 cup fresh or frozen blueberries, thawed
  and well drained

OVEN 350°   1 LOAF

In large mixer bowl, combine all ingredients except blueberries. Mix at low speed until blended; beat at medium speed 2 minutes. Stir in blueberries. Turn into 9x5-inch loaf pan, which has been greased on the bottom only. Bake at 350° for 60 to 70 minutes, until toothpick inserted in center comes out clean. Cool 10 minutes; remove from pan. Frost with Orange Frosting, page 12, if desired. Cool completely before slicing.

Tip: For blueberry muffins, fill greased muffin cups ⅔ full. Bake at 350° for 25 to 30 minutes. Makes about 18 muffins.

*For use with Pillsbury's Best Self-Rising Flour, omit baking powder and salt.

HIGH ALTITUDE ADJUSTMENT — 5,200 FEET. Reduce baking powder to 1½ teaspoons. Line bottom of loaf pan with greased, waxed paper.

The spicy fragrance of this recipe can be enjoyed two ways — as a coffee cake or as muffins. A genuinely good-tasting coffee treat that can be ready in about an hour.

Spicy Apple Crunch Cake

    2 cups Pillsbury's Best All Purpose Flour*
    1 cup firmly packed brown sugar
    1 teaspoon baking powder
    1 teaspoon soda
    1 teaspoon salt
    1 teaspoon cinnamon
    ¼ teaspoon cloves
    ½ cup cooking oil
    2 eggs
    1 cup applesauce
    ¼ cup milk
    1 cup chopped walnuts

Topping

    ½ cup firmly packed brown sugar
    ½ cup chopped walnuts
    ¼ cup Pillsbury's Best All Purpose or
       Self-Rising Flour
    3 tablespoons butter or margarine, softened
    1 teaspoon cinnamon

OVEN 350°   13X9-INCH COFFEE CAKE

In large mixer bowl, combine all ingredients except walnuts. Blend at low speed until moistened; beat 3 minutes at medium speed. Stir in walnuts. Pour batter into 13x9-inch pan, which has been greased on the bottom only. Sprinkle on Topping. Bake at 350° for 35 to 40 minutes or until toothpick inserted in center comes out clean. Serve warm or cold.

Topping: In small mixing bowl, combine all ingredients. Mix until well blended.

Tip: For muffins, fill paper-lined muffin cups, two-thirds full. Sprinkle on Topping. Bake at 350° for 20 to 25 minutes. Makes about 24 muffins.

*For use with Pillsbury's Best Self-Rising Flour, omit baking powder and salt; reduce soda to ½ teaspoon.

HIGH ALTITUDE ADJUSTMENT — 5,200 FEET.
Reduce baking powder to ½ teaspoon and soda to ½ teaspoon.

The old-fashioned goodness of corn bread done to perfection in this 45-minute-to-make recipe. Serve it warm and pass the butter.

Maryland Corn Bread

    1 cup Pillsbury's Best All Purpose Flour*
    1 cup cornmeal
    3 tablespoons sugar
    2 teaspoons baking powder
    1 teaspoon salt
    1 egg
    1 cup milk
    ¼ cup shortening, melted, or cooking oil

OVEN 400°   8-INCH CORN BREAD

In large mixing bowl, combine flour, cornmeal, sugar, baking powder and salt. Combine egg, milk and melted shortening. Add to dry ingredients; stir until all dry particles are moistened. Pour into well-greased 8-inch square pan. Bake at 400° for 25 to 30 minutes until golden brown. Serve warm, cut in squares.

*For use with Pillsbury's Best Self-Rising Flour, omit baking powder and salt.

HIGH ALTITUDE ADJUSTMENT — 5,200 FEET.
Reduce baking powder to 1 teaspoon.

MENU

Apres Ski Party
Beef Stew
Maryland Cornbread with
Honey Butter (Page 14)
Gelatin Fruit Salad
Pumpkin Pie
Beverage

Oatmeal gives color and bite to this pretty round coffee cake. An orangy-pecan topping adds a crunchy touch. Make it in less than an hour.

Pecan Sunrise Bread

1½ cups Pillsbury's Best All Purpose Flour*
¾ cup sugar
1½ teaspoons baking powder
½ teaspoon soda
½ teaspoon salt
½ cup rolled oats
¾ cup milk
⅓ cup shortening
2 eggs
¼ cup pecan halves
⅓ cup sugar
2 tablespoons butter or margarine
1 tablespoon grated orange peel

OVEN 375°   9-INCH COFFEE CAKE

In large mixer bowl, combine flour, ¾ cup sugar, baking powder, soda, salt, rolled oats, milk, shortening and eggs. Blend at low speed until thoroughly mixed. Spread in greased 9-inch round layer or square pan. Arrange pecan halves on top of batter. Blend ⅓ cup sugar, butter and orange peel until mixture resembles coarse crumbs. Sprinkle evenly over batter. Bake at 375° for 30 to 35 minutes until toothpick inserted in center comes out clean. Serve warm.

*For use with Pillsbury's Best Self-Rising Flour, omit baking powder and salt; decrease soda to ¼ teaspoon.

Ring around your family's heart with this coffee cake that's holiday good, everyday easy. And, it's ready in an hour.

Jiffy Mince Coffee Ring

2 cups Pillsbury's Best All Purpose Flour*
¾ cup sugar
2½ teaspoons baking powder
½ teaspoon salt
⅓ cup shortening
1 egg, slightly beaten
½ cup milk
¾ cup prepared mincemeat
Chopped walnuts, if desired

OVEN 375°   9-INCH COFFEE RING

In large mixing bowl, combine flour, sugar, baking powder and salt. Cut in shortening until mixture is crumbly. Combine egg, milk and mincemeat. Add to dry ingredients; mix only until dry particles are moistened. Spoon into well-greased 9-inch ring mold. Bake at 375° for 30 to 35 minutes, until toothpick inserted in center comes out clean. Frost with Vanilla Frosting, page 12. Sprinkle with nuts.

*For use with Pillsbury's Best Self-Rising Flour, omit baking powder and salt.

*HIGH ALTITUDE ADJUSTMENT — 5,200 FEET.
Reduce baking powder to 1½ teaspoons.*

Here's a coffee-treat for breakfast or dessert . . . in a raisin-orange-nut cake that is mouth-watering moist. An easy-do in forty-five minutes.

Royal Danish Kuchen

2 cups Pillsbury's Best All Purpose Flour*
1 cup sugar
1½ teaspoons baking powder
1 teaspoon salt
½ teaspoon soda
1 teaspoon cinnamon
¼ teaspoon nutmeg
1 cup raisins
1 tablespoon grated orange peel
1 cup buttermilk or sour milk
⅓ cup cooking oil
1 egg
½ cup sugar
½ cup chopped nuts
1 teaspoon cinnamon
2 tablespoons butter or margarine

OVEN 375°   9-INCH COFFEE CAKE

In large mixing bowl, combine flour, sugar, baking powder, salt, soda, cinnamon, nutmeg, raisins and orange peel. Add buttermilk, oil and egg. Stir until smooth and well blended. Pour into greased 9-inch square pan. Combine sugar, nuts and cinnamon; sprinkle over batter. Dot with butter. Bake at 375° for 30 to 35 minutes until toothpick inserted in center comes out clean. Serve warm or cold.

*For use with Pillsbury's Best Self-Rising Flour, omit baking powder, salt and soda.

*HIGH ALTITUDE ADJUSTMENT — 5,200 FEET.
Reduce baking powder to ¾ teaspoon.*

Two traditional favorites — apples and Cheddar cheese — blend together in the newest and most fun party bread. Make it in 1½ hours, but it's best the next day.

Peppy Apple-Cheese Bread

   2 cups Pillsbury's Best All Purpose Flour*
  ⅔ cup sugar
   1 teaspoon baking powder
  ½ teaspoon soda
  ½ teaspoon salt
  ½ cup shortening
   2 eggs
1½ cups pared, shredded apple
  ½ cup shredded Cheddar cheese
  ½ cup chopped walnuts

OVEN 350°   1 LOAF

In large mixing bowl, combine flour, sugar, baking powder, soda, salt, shortening and eggs. Mix until well blended. Stir in shredded apple, Cheddar cheese and chopped walnuts; mix well. Turn into well-greased 9x5-inch loaf pan. Bake at 350° for 50 to 60 minutes, until toothpick inserted in center comes out clean. Remove from pan. Cool thoroughly before slicing.

*For use with Pillsbury's Best Self-Rising Flour, omit baking powder, soda and salt.

HIGH ALTITUDE ADJUSTMENT — 5,200 FEET. Reduce baking powder to ½ teaspoon and soda to ¼ teaspoon.

Graham cracker crumbs give this brown bread a sweet nutty flavor. Takes a little over an hour to bake.

Graham Cracker Brown Bread

1¾ cups Pillsbury's Best All Purpose Flour*
2 cups graham cracker crumbs
2 teaspoons soda
1 teaspoon salt
1 teaspoon nutmeg
½ cup shortening
¾ cup molasses
2 eggs
1¾ cups buttermilk or sour milk
1 cup raisins

OVEN 350°   1 LARGE LOAF

In large mixer bowl, combine all ingredients except raisins. Mix at low speed until moistened; beat 2 minutes at medium speed. Stir in raisins. Turn batter into 9x5-inch loaf pan, which has been greased on the bottom only. Bake at 350° for 65 to 70 minutes, until toothpick inserted in center comes out clean. Remove from pan. Cool thoroughly before slicing.

*For use with Pillsbury's Best Self Rising Flour, increase flour to 2 cups; decrease soda to 1 teaspoon and salt to ½ teaspoon.

HIGH ALTITUDE ADJUSTMENT — 5,200 FEET.
Reduce soda to 1 teaspoon. Line bottom of pan with greased, waxed paper. Bake at 400° for 65 to 70 minutes.

A prune quick bread enhanced with cinnamon and nutmeg. Pull it sweet-smelling from the oven in one hour. Stores well, too.

Easy Prune Loaf

2 cups Pillsbury's Best All Purpose Flour*
1 cup sugar
3 teaspoons baking powder
1 teaspoon salt
½ teaspoon cinnamon
½ teaspoon nutmeg
¼ teaspoon cloves
1 cup water
½ cup shortening
2 eggs
1 cup finely cut-up cooked prunes

OVEN 375°   1 LOAF

In large mixer bowl, combine all ingredients except prunes. Blend at low speed until dry ingredients are moistened. Beat at medium speed 3 minutes. Stir in prunes. Turn into 9x5-inch loaf pan, which has been greased on the bottom only. Bake at 375° for 50 to 60 minutes, until toothpick inserted in center comes out clean. Cool thoroughly before slicing.

*For use with Pillsbury's Best Self-Rising Flour, increase flour to 2½ cups and omit baking powder and salt.

HIGH ALTITUDE ADJUSTMENT — 5,200 FEET.
Reduce baking powder to 1½ teaspoons. Line bottom of pan with greased, waxed paper.

A quick nut loaf with an English tradition of honey and spice. Best the next day.

English Honey Loaf

2¼ cups Pillsbury's Best All Purpose Flour*
1 cup sugar
1 teaspoon baking powder
1 teaspoon salt
¾ teaspoon soda
½ teaspoon cinnamon
½ teaspoon cloves
½ teaspoon allspice
¼ teaspoon ginger
1½ teaspoons grated lemon peel
½ cup raisins
½ cup chopped walnuts
⅓ cup shortening
⅓ cup honey
½ cup strong cold coffee
2 eggs

OVEN 350°   1 LOAF

In large mixer bowl, combine all ingredients. Blend until moistened. Beat 2 minutes at low speed. Turn into well-greased 9x5-inch loaf pan. Bake at 350° for 55 to 60 minutes, until toothpick inserted in center comes out clean. Cool thoroughly before slicing.

*Not recommended for use with Pillsbury's Best Self-Rising Flour.

HIGH ALTITUDE ADJUSTMENT — 5,200 FEET.
Reduce baking powder to ½ teaspoon and soda to ¼ teaspoon.

All the moist richness of a steamed nut bread, but this is baked in the oven . . . in cans. Sliced rounds of this rich dark bread are good warm or cold. Prepare in an hour and a half.

Date-Rich Bran Bread

    2 cups Pillsbury's Best All Purpose Flour*
    ¾ cup firmly packed brown sugar
    2 teaspoons soda
    ½ teaspoon salt
    1½ cups bran flakes
     1 cup cut-up dates
    ½ cup chopped pecans
    1½ cups buttermilk or sour milk

OVEN 350°   3 SMALL LOAVES

In large mixing bowl, combine all ingredients except buttermilk. Add buttermilk and mix well. Spoon into 3 well-greased No. 2 cans. Cover tops of cans with aluminum foil. Bake at 350° for 60 to 70 minutes, until top springs back when lightly touched in center. Remove from cans immediately. Serve warm or cold.

Tips: No. 2 cans hold approximately 1½ cups liquid.

If desired, cover and bake in two 4-cup molds.

*For use with Pillsbury's Best Self-Rising Flour, decrease soda to 1 teaspoon and omit salt.
HIGH ALTITUDE ADJUSTMENT — 5,200 FEET. Reduce soda to 1 teaspoon.

If you have canned peaches, cherries and nuts on hand, you're ready to make this colorful one-bowl quick bread. Slices best the next day, though.

Peachy Nut Bread

    2 cups Pillsbury's Best All Purpose Flour*
    ⅔ cup sugar
     1 teaspoon baking powder
    ½ teaspoon soda
    ½ teaspoon salt
     1 tablespoon grated orange peel
    ⅓ cup shortening
    ¼ cup buttermilk or sour milk
    2 eggs
     1 cup (1 lb. can) mashed, drained canned
        peaches
    ½ cup chopped nuts
    ¼ cup chopped maraschino cherries

OVEN 350°   1 LOAF

In large mixer bowl, combine all ingredients except nuts and cherries. Blend well at medium speed. Stir in nuts and cherries. Pour into 9x5-inch loaf pan, which has been greased on the bottom only. Bake at 350° for 50 to 60 minutes until a toothpick inserted in center comes out clean. Remove from pan. Cool thoroughly before slicing.

*For use with Pillsbury's Best Self-Rising Flour, omit baking powder, soda and salt.
HIGH ALTITUDE ADJUSTMENT — 5,200 FEET. Line bottom of pan with greased, waxed paper.

An ambrosia of flavors: banana, coconut and orange mingle in this moist, fine-textured nut bread. Perfect for your next luncheon — and it's best made the day before.

Aloha Banana Bread

    2 cups Pillsbury's Best All Purpose Flour*
     1 cup sugar
     1 teaspoon soda
    ½ teaspoon salt
    ½ cup butter or margarine, softened
    2 eggs
    ¼ cup milk
     1 cup (2 medium) mashed ripe banana
     1 tablespoon grated orange peel
     1 teaspoon vanilla
    ½ teaspoon almond extract
     1 cup flaked coconut
    ½ cup chopped nuts

OVEN 350°   1 LOAF

In large mixer bowl, combine all ingredients except coconut and nuts. Blend at low speed until dry ingredients are moistened. Beat at medium speed 3 minutes. Stir in coconut and nuts. Turn into 9x5-inch loaf pan, which has been greased on the bottom only. Bake at 350° for 60 to 70 minutes, until toothpick inserted in center comes out clean. Remove from pan immediately. Cool thoroughly before slicing.

*For use with Pillsbury's Best Self-Rising Flour, increase flour to 2¼ cups and omit soda and salt.

Give a lift to luncheon with this moist banana and nut loaf. Easy to serve when made the day before.

Banana Luncheon Bread

   2 cups Pillsbury's Best All Purpose Flour*
    1 cup sugar
    1 teaspoon baking powder
    1 teaspoon salt
  ½ teaspoon soda
  ½ cup shortening
    1 cup (2 medium) mashed ripe banana
    2 eggs
  ½ cup chopped walnuts

OVEN 350°   1 LOAF

In large mixer bowl, combine all ingredients except walnuts. Blend well at medium speed. Stir in walnuts. Pour into 9x5-inch loaf pan, which has been greased on the bottom only. Bake at 350° for 65 to 75 minutes until toothpick inserted in center comes out clean. Remove from pan; cool thoroughly before slicing.

*For use with Pillsbury's Best Self-Rising Flour, increase flour to 2¼ cups; omit baking powder, salt and soda.

HIGH ALTITUDE ADJUSTMENT — 5,200 FEET. Reduce baking powder to ½ teaspoon and soda to ¼ teaspoon.

Quick coffee cake from mix that takes less than I hour. Cranberry-orange relish makes a colorful and tasty topping.

Cranberry Crisscross Coffee Cake

    I package Pillsbury Cinnamon Streusel
        Coffee Cake Mix
    I package (I0 oz.) frozen cranberry-orange
        relish, thawed and drained thoroughly
  ⅓ cup chopped walnuts

OVEN 375°   8-INCH COFFEE CAKE

Prepare coffee cake mix as directed on package, spreading half of batter in greased and lightly floured 8 or 9-inch square pan. Combine ½ cup of topping mix with relish and nuts; spread over batter. Cover with remaining batter and sprinkle with remaining topping mix. Bake at 375° for 35 to 40 minutes until cake springs back when lightly touched in center. Serve warm or cold.

A quick coffee cake, glistening with jewel-like mandarin oranges hidden in the crumb topping. Quickly whipped together in an hour and a quarter.

Mandarin Coffee Cake

  2 cups Pillsbury's Best All Purpose Flour*
    I cup sugar
2½ teaspoons baking powder
    I teaspoon salt
  ½ teaspoon nutmeg
  ½ cup butter or margarine, softened
  ¾ cup milk
    I egg
    I teaspoon vanilla
    I can (II oz.) mandarin oranges, drained

OVEN 350°   9-INCH COFFEE CAKE

In large mixing bowl, combine flour, sugar, baking powder, salt and nutmeg. With pastry blender, cut in butter until particles are fine. Reserve ½ cup crumb mixture for topping. Add milk, egg and vanilla to remaining crumb mixture; mix well. Spread in 9-inch square pan, which has been greased on the bottom only. Arrange mandarin oranges in rows on top. Sprinkle on reserved crumb mixture. Bake at

350° for 40 to 45 minutes until top springs back when touched lightly in center.

*For use with Pillsbury's Best Self-Rising Flour, increase flour to 2¼ cups; omit baking powder and salt.

HIGH ALTITUDE ADJUSTMENT — 5,200 FEET. Reduce baking powder to I½ teaspoons.

Rich, moist cinnamon coffee cake hides a layer of nutty brown sugar filling. Plus a topping of more nutty brown sugar. Ready in I hour.

Cinnamon Crunch Coffee Cake

  2 cups Pillsbury's Best All Purpose Flour*
  ¾ cup sugar
  3 teaspoons baking powder
    I teaspoon cinnamon
  ½ teaspoon salt
  ¼ teaspoon nutmeg
  ⅓ cup shortening
    I cup milk
    2 eggs

<u>Crumb Mixture</u>
  ⅔ cup firmly packed brown sugar
  2 tablespoons flour
  2 tablespoons butter or margarine, softened
    I cup chopped pecans

OVEN 350°   9-INCH COFFEE CAKE

In large mixer bowl, combine all ingredients except Crumb Mixture. Beat 3 minutes at medium speed. Pour half of batter into greased and floured 9-inch square pan. Sprinkle two-thirds of Crumb Mixture over batter in pan. Cover with remaining batter and top with remaining Crumb Mixture. Bake at 350° for 30 to 40 minutes until toothpick inserted in center comes out clean. Serve warm.

<u>Crumb Mixture</u>: In small bowl, combine brown sugar and flour. Cut in butter until mixture is crumbly; stir in pecans.

*For use with Pillsbury's Best Self-Rising Flour, omit baking powder and salt.

HIGH ALTITUDE ADJUSTMENT — 5,200 FEET. Reduce baking powder to I½ teaspoons. Bake at 375° for 30 to 40 minutes.

A moist peanut butter coffee cake with a creamy smooth brown sugar topping. Really quick and easy to make.

Peanut Butter Brunch Cake

1½ cups Pillsbury's Best All Purpose Flour*
¾ cup sugar
2 teaspoons baking powder
½ teaspoon salt
1 egg
⅔ cup milk
¼ cup shortening
⅓ cup peanut butter
½ cup chopped nuts
½ cup dairy sour cream
¼ cup firmly packed brown sugar

OVEN 350°   9-INCH COFFEE CAKE

In large mixer bowl, combine all ingredients except nuts, sour cream and brown sugar. Blend at lowest speed until moistened; beat 3 minutes at medium speed. Stir in nuts. Spread in 9-inch square pan, which has been greased on the bottom only.

In small mixing bowl, combine sour cream and brown sugar. Mix well; spread over batter. Bake at 350° for 35 to 40 minutes until cake springs back when touched lightly in center. Serve warm.

*For use with Pillsbury's Best Self-Rising Flour, omit baking powder and salt.

HIGH ALTITUDE ADJUSTMENT — 5,200 FEET. Reduce baking powder to 1 teaspoon.

Hawaiian-flavored treat in 45 minutes. Start with refrigerated crescent dough for a lush and easy coffee cake.

Honey Ambrosia Coffee Cake

⅔ cup flaked coconut
⅔ cup drained crushed pineapple
⅓ cup honey
¼ cup butter or margarine, softened
2 cans Pillsbury Refrigerated Quick Crescent Dinner Rolls

OVEN 375°   9-INCH COFFEE CAKE

In small mixing bowl, combine coconut, pineapple, honey and butter. Unwrap crescent dough; separate into 16 triangles. Place 1 tablespoon of pineapple mixture on wide end of crescent triangle. Spread over about half of triangle. Roll up each triangle, starting at wide end of triangle and rolling to opposite point. Place rolls in two rows, point-side down, in greased 9-inch square pan. Bake at 375° for 25 to 30 minutes until golden brown and center is done. Cool slightly. Cut into squares.

Tip: If desired, remove from pan immediately after removing from oven and place right-side up on serving plate.

A kicky combination of cornmeal, mincemeat and molasses for an unusually delicious, moist brown bread. Best the next day.

Merry Mince Brown Bread

2 cups cornmeal
1½ cups Pillsbury's Best All Purpose Flour*
2 teaspoons soda
1 teaspoon salt
2 cups milk
1 cup prepared mincemeat
¾ cup dark molasses

OVEN 350°   4 SMALL LOAVES

In large mixing bowl, combine all ingredients; mix well. Divide batter into 4 well-greased No. 2 cans, filling ⅔ full. Cover tightly with aluminum foil. Bake at 350° for 60 to 65 minutes until top springs back when touched lightly. Cool 10 minutes. Remove from cans. Cool completely.

Tips: A well-greased 2-quart ring mold may be substituted for cans.

No. 2 cans contain about 1 lb. 4 oz. and hold 2½ cups liquid.

*For use with Pillsbury's Best Self-Rising Flour, omit soda and salt.

HIGH ALTITUDE ADJUSTMENT — 5,200 FEET. Reduce soda to 1 teaspoon.

Shades of an old Dutch kitchen. Applesauce and spice add a rich autumn flavor to this nut bread.

Pennsylvania Applesauce Bread

    2 cups Pillsbury's Best All Purpose Flour*
    ¾ cup sugar
    I teaspoon baking powder
    I teaspoon soda
    I teaspoon salt
    I teaspoon cinnamon
    ½ teaspoon nutmeg
    I teaspoon vanilla
    ½ cup shortening
    I cup applesauce
    2 eggs
    ½ cup chopped nuts

OVEN 350°   I LOAF

In large mixer bowl, combine all ingredients except nuts. Beat at medium speed until well blended. Stir in nuts. Pour into 9x5-inch loaf pan which has been greased on the bottom only. Bake at 350° for 55 to 60 minutes until toothpick inserted in center comes out clean. Loosen edges with spatula; remove from pan. Cool thoroughly before slicing.

*For use with Pillsbury's Best Self-Rising Flour, omit baking powder, soda and salt.

HIGH ALTITUDE ADJUSTMENT — 5,200 FEET.
Reduce baking powder to ½ teaspoon and soda to ½ teaspoon.

Crunchy bacon chips and chopped salted peanuts top this homey cornbread. It bakes up in about 15 minutes.

Southern Bacon Brunchers

    ½ lb. (10 strips) bacon
    1¼ cups Pillsbury's Best All Purpose Flour*
    ¾ cup cornmeal
    ¼ cup sugar
    3 teaspoons baking powder
    ½ teaspoon salt
    I cup milk
    I egg
    ¼ cup bacon drippings
    ½ cup chopped salted peanuts

OVEN 450°   9-INCH CORNBREAD

Fry bacon until crisp; reserve ¼ cup bacon drippings. Cool and crumble bacon; set aside. In large mixing bowl, combine flour, cornmeal, sugar, baking powder and salt. Combine

milk, egg and bacon drippings. Add to dry ingredients and stir only until all dry particles are moistened. Spread batter in greased 9-inch square pan. Sprinkle on peanuts and crumbled bacon. Bake at 450° for 15 to 18 minutes, until top springs back when touched lightly in center. Serve hot.

Tips: To eliminate frying bacon, use 4 to 6 tablespoons bacon-flavored bits for the crumbled bacon. Substitute cooking oil for bacon drippings and increase salt to ¾ teaspoon.

If desired, bake in a greased 15x10-inch jelly roll pan at 450° for 10 to 12 minutes.

*For use with Pillsbury's Best Self-Rising Flour, omit baking powder and salt.

HIGH ALTITUDE ADJUSTMENT — 5,200 FEET.
Reduce baking powder to 1½ teaspoons.

Add raisins for sweetness, walnuts for crunch, buttermilk for creamy richness, cinnamon and cloves for spice. Ummmm. Prepare it in an hour.

Old Country Raisin Loaf

    3 cups Pillsbury's Best All Purpose Flour*
    I cup firmly packed brown sugar
    2 teaspoons soda
    1½ teaspoons salt
    I teaspoon cinnamon
    ¼ teaspoon cloves
    ½ cup shortening
    1½ cups buttermilk or sour milk
    I egg
    I cup raisins
    ½ cup chopped walnuts

OVEN 350°   2 LOAVES

In large mixer bowl, combine all ingredients except raisins and nuts. Blend well. Stir in remaining ingredients. Pour into two greased 9x5-inch loaf pans. Bake at 350° for 40 to 50 minutes until toothpick inserted in center comes out clean. Cool 5 to 10 minutes before removing from pans. Cool completely before slicing.

Tip: For small round loaves, bake batter in two greased No. 2 cans and one greased 9x5-inch loaf pan.

*Pillsbury's Best Self-Rising Flour is not recommended for use in this recipe.

HIGH ALTITUDE ADJUSTMENT — 5,200 FEET.
Reduce soda to 1½ teaspoons. Line bottom of pan with greased, waxed paper.

Old-world German cake. Moist, tender coffee cake dappled with peaches, sprinkled with crunchy crumbs. Serve warm in less than an hour.

Kwik Peach Kuchen

2 cups Pillsbury's Best All Purpose Flour*
½ cup sugar
3 teaspoons baking powder
½ teaspoon salt
1 package active dry yeast
½ cup shortening
½ cup milk
2 eggs
¼ teaspoon lemon extract
1 can (1 lb. 13 oz.) peach slices, drained

Topping

½ cup firmly packed brown sugar
¼ cup Pillsbury's Best All Purpose or
   Self-Rising Flour
½ teaspoon cinnamon
2 tablespoons butter or margarine
¼ cup chopped nuts

OVEN 350°   13X9-INCH KUCHEN

In large mixer bowl, combine flour, sugar, baking powder, salt and dry yeast. Add shortening, milk, eggs and lemon extract. Blend at lowest speed until moistened; beat 2 minutes at medium speed. Spread over bottom of greased 13x9-inch pan. Arrange peach slices on top, pressing in slightly. Sprinkle with Topping. Bake at 350° for 30 to 35 minutes until golden brown. Serve warm or cold.

Topping: Combine brown sugar, flour and cinnamon. Cut in butter until crumbly. Mix in nuts.

Tip: The tiny speckles of yeast in the batter disappear during baking.

*For use with Pillsbury's Best Self-Rising Flour, omit baking powder and salt.
HIGH ALTITUDE ADJUSTMENT — 5,200 FEET. Reduce baking powder to 1½ teaspoons.

Puffy-proud little spicy muffins, with a hidden jam surprise inside. Serve them warm in 45 minutes.

Jam-Dandy Muffins

1⅔ cups Pillsbury's Best All Purpose Flour*
½ cup sugar
2 teaspoons baking powder
½ teaspoon salt
⅛ teaspoon nutmeg or cinnamon
⅓ cup shortening
¾ cup milk
1 egg
Apricot jam
Chopped nuts

OVEN 400°   12 MUFFINS

In mixing bowl, combine flour, sugar, baking powder, salt and nutmeg. Cut in shortening until particles are fine. Add milk and egg; mix just until thoroughly blended. Spoon into greased muffin cups. Place 1 teaspoon jam on top of each muffin, pressing into batter slightly. Sprinkle with a few chopped nuts. Bake at 400° for 20 to 25 minutes until tops spring back when touched lightly. Serve warm.

Tip: Other flavors of jam or marmalade may be used.

*Not recommended for use with Pillsbury's Best Self-Rising Flour.

HIGH ALTITUDE ADJUSTMENT — 5,200 FEET. Reduce baking powder to 1 teaspoon.

A creamy onion-type bread. Good served with a salad for lunch or with meats at dinner time — ready in about an hour.

Onion Patch Pudding

  2 cups chopped onion
¼ cup butter or margarine
  I egg, well beaten
  I tablespoon dried parsley flakes
½ teaspoon salt
⅛ teaspoon pepper
2¼ cups Pillsbury's Best All Purpose Flour*
  3 teaspoons baking powder
  I teaspoon salt
¼ cup butter or margarine
¾ cup milk

Sour Cream Topping
1½ cups dairy sour cream
  2 eggs
½ teaspoon salt
⅛ teaspoon pepper

OVEN 375°   9 SERVINGS

In 9-inch square pan, sauté chopped onion in butter over medium heat. Remove from heat; stir in egg, parsley, salt and pepper. Spread evenly over bottom of pan. In large mixing bowl, combine flour, baking powder and salt. With pastry blender, cut in butter until particles are fine. Add milk all at once, stirring just until dry particles are moistened. Knead on floured surface 10 to 12 times. Pat or roll out to a 9-inch square; place over onion mixture. Pour Sour Cream Topping over dough. Bake at 375° for 40 to 45 minutes until golden brown. Serve hot, cut in squares.

Sour Cream Topping: In small mixing bowl, combine all ingredients; mix well.

*For use with Pillsbury's Best Self-Rising Flour, omit baking powder and salt in biscuit dough.

MENU
Sunday Night Supper
Sliced Cold Beef
Onion Patch Pudding
Relishes
Peaches and Cookies
Beverage

Tender orange muffins that feature a spicy streusel topping — ready in less than an hour!

Orange Streusel Muffins

  2 cups Pillsbury's Best All Purpose Flour*
⅓ cup sugar
  3 teaspoons baking powder
  I teaspoon salt
½ cup chopped pecans
  I egg
  I tablespoon grated orange peel
½ cup orange juice
½ cup orange marmalade or pineapple
   preserves
¼ cup milk
¼ cup cooking oil

Topping
¼ cup sugar
  I tablespoon flour
  I tablespoon butter or margarine, softened
½ teaspoon cinnamon
¼ teaspoon nutmeg

OVEN 400°   12 LARGE MUFFINS

In large mixing bowl, combine flour, sugar, baking powder, salt and chopped pecans. Combine egg, orange peel, orange juice, orange marmalade, milk and oil. Add to dry ingredients. Mix only until all dry particles are moistened. Fill muffin cups, that have been lined with paper baking cups, two-thirds full. Prepare Topping. Sprinkle Topping over muffins. Bake at 400° for 20 to 25 minutes until golden brown. Serve warm.

Topping: In small mixing bowl, combine all ingredients.

*For use with Pillsbury's Best Self-Rising Flour, omit baking powder and salt.

HIGH ALTITUDE ADJUSTMENT — 5,200 FEET. Reduce baking powder to 1½ teaspoons.

Make popovers with savory cheese flavor, golden brown and buttery. A lively addition to your next luncheon. Serve hot from the oven for best flavor.

Cheese Popover Puffs

  I cup Pillsbury's Best All Purpose Flour*
½ teaspoon salt
  I cup milk
  I tablespoon butter or margarine, melted
  2 eggs
¼ cup shredded Cheddar cheese

OVEN 425°   6 TO 8 POPOVERS

In small mixing bowl, combine flour, salt, milk, butter and eggs. Beat with rotary beater until smooth. Stir in cheese. Pour into greased pop-over pan or muffin cups, filling two-thirds full. Bake at 425° for 15 minutes, then reduce oven temperature to 350° and bake 35 minutes longer until golden brown. Prick with a sharp knife during last 5 minutes of baking to allow for escape of steam. Serve immediately.

*Pillsbury's Best Self-Rising Flour is not recommended for use in this recipe.

HIGH ALTITUDE ADJUSTMENT — 5,200 FEET.
Bake at 450° for 15 minutes, then reduce oven temperature to 350° for 25 minutes.

Spicy banana muffins dressed up with a jam center. Vary the jams and arrange a pretty breakfast tray. Serve 'em hot from the oven in just a half hour.

Little Miss Muffins

> 2 cups Pillsbury's Best All Purpose Flour*
> ½ cup sugar
> 2 teaspoons baking powder
> I teaspoon salt
> ½ teaspoon soda
> ¼ teaspoon nutmeg
> I cup (2 medium) mashed ripe banana
> I egg
> ⅓ cup milk
> ⅓ cup cooking oil
> Jam or preserves

OVEN 375°   I2 MUFFINS

In large mixing bowl, combine all ingredients except jam. Mix until dry ingredients are moistened. Fill well-greased muffin cups two-thirds full. With a teaspoon, make a slight indentation in the center of each and fill with a teaspoon of jam. Bake at 375° for I8 to 20 minutes until golden brown. Serve warm.

*For use with Pillsbury's Best Self-Rising Flour, increase flour to 2¼ cups; omit baking powder, salt and soda.

HIGH ALTITUDE ADJUSTMENT — 5,200 FEET. Reduce baking powder to ¼ teaspoon and soda to ¼ teaspoon. Bake at 375° for 20 to 25 minutes.

Homemade doughnuts at their best. Sugared or glazed to suit your taste.

Country Kitchen Doughnuts

> 4⅔ cups Pillsbury's Best All Purpose Flour*
> I cup sugar
> 2 teaspoons baking powder
> I teaspoon soda
> I teaspoon salt
> I teaspoon grated lemon peel
> ½ teaspoon nutmeg
> I cup buttermilk or sour milk
> ¼ cup butter or margarine, melted
> I teaspoon lemon extract
> 2 eggs

DEEP FAT 375°   ABOUT 24 DOUGHNUTS

In large mixing bowl, combine flour, sugar, baking powder, soda, salt, lemon peel and nutmeg. Combine buttermilk, butter, lemon extract and eggs. Add to dry ingredients; mix until well blended. If desired, chill dough for easier handling. Toss dough on well-floured surface until no longer sticky; roll out on well-floured surface to ¼-inch thickness. Cut with 3-inch doughnut cutter. Fry in deep, hot fat (375°) I to 2 minutes on each side, until golden brown. Drain on absorbent paper. Roll in sugar or glaze.

*For use with Pillsbury's Best Self-Rising Flour, omit baking powder, soda and salt.

HIGH ALTITUDE ADJUSTMENT — 5,200 FEET. Reduce baking powder to I teaspoon.

Rich, holiday flavor, any time of the year. Tender muffins topped with ready-made mincemeat and crumbs. Bake them up in less than an hour.

Mince Crowned Muffins

<u>Muffins</u>

> 2 cups Pillsbury's Best All Purpose Flour*
> ⅓ cup sugar
> 3 teaspoons baking powder
> ½ teaspoon salt
> ¼ cup cooking oil or shortening, melted
> I cup milk
> I egg, slightly beaten
> ½ cup prepared mincemeat

<u>Topping</u>

> ¼ cup Pillsbury's Best All Purpose or
>   Self-Rising Flour
> ¼ cup firmly packed brown sugar
> ¼ teaspoon cinnamon
> 2 tablespoons chopped nuts
> I tablespoon butter or margarine, melted

OVEN 375°   I2 MUFFINS

<u>Muffins:</u> In large mixing bowl, combine flour, sugar, baking powder and salt. Add oil, milk and egg. Stir only until dry particles are moistened. Fill greased muffin cups three-fourths full. Press I teaspoon prepared mincemeat into center of each with back of spoon. Sprinkle Topping over center of muffins. Bake at 375° for 20 to 25 minutes until golden brown.

<u>Topping:</u> In small mixing bowl, combine all ingredients; mix well.

*For use with Pillsbury's Best Self-Rising Flour, increase flour to 2⅓ cups; omit baking powder and salt.

HIGH ALTITUDE ADJUSTMENT — 5,200 FEET. Reduce baking powder to 1½ teaspoons.

Moist, dark and tender! An apricot-raisin bread with a hint of orange that tastes even better the second day.

Holiday Treat

1½ cups apricot nectar
1½ cups raisins
⅓ cup (about 12) cut-up dried apricots
1 tablespoon grated orange peel
2¾ cups Pillsbury's Best All Purpose Flour*
1 cup sugar
2 teaspoons soda
1 teaspoon salt
1 tablespoon shortening
1 egg
⅓ cup light cream
½ cup chopped walnuts

OVEN 350°   4 SMALL LOAVES

In large saucepan, combine apricot nectar, raisins, dried apricots and orange peel. Simmer for 5 minutes. Cool. In large mixer bowl, combine cooled fruit mixture and remaining ingredients. Mix at low speed 3 minutes, until well blended. Turn into 4 well-greased No. 2 cans. Bake at 350° for 50 to 60 minutes until toothpick inserted in center comes out clean. Remove from cans. Cool before slicing.

Tips: No. 2 cans hold approximately 1½ cups of liquid.

Bread may be baked in a well-greased 9x5-inch loaf pan at 325° for 80 to 90 minutes.

*For use with Pillsbury's Best Self-Rising Flour, decrease soda to ½ teaspoon and omit salt.

As merry as the cranberry! A pretty Christmas loaf is this festive cranberry, orange and nut bread. It stores well.

Holiday Cranberry Bread

      2 cups Pillsbury's Best All Purpose Flour*
      1 cup sugar
   1½ teaspoons baking powder
      1 teaspoon salt
      ½ teaspoon soda
      ¾ cup orange juice
      1 tablespoon grated orange peel
      2 tablespoons shortening
      1 egg
      1 cup fresh or frozen cranberries, chopped
         or halved
      1 cup chopped nuts

OVEN 350°   1 LOAF

In large mixing bowl, combine flour, sugar, baking powder, salt and soda. Stir to mix well. Add orange juice, orange peel, shortening and egg to dry ingredients. Mix until well blended. Stir in cranberries and chopped nuts. Turn into 9x5-inch loaf pan, which has been greased on the bottom only. Bake at 350° for 55 to 65 minutes, until toothpick inserted in center comes out clean. Cool thoroughly before slicing.

*For use with Pillsbury's Best Self-Rising Flour, omit baking powder, salt and soda.

*HIGH ALTITUDE ADJUSTMENT — 5,200 FEET.
Reduce baking powder to ¾ teaspoon and soda to ¼ teaspoon.*

121

Tart and tangy combination of apricots and orange in a new-fashioned nut bread. Plan on an hour and a half from start to finish.

Nutty Apricot Snack Loaf

    I cup dried apricots
    2 cups Pillsbury's Best All Purpose Flour*
    I cup sugar
    2 teaspoons baking powder
    I teaspoon salt
    ¼ teaspoon soda
    ¼ cup shortening
    I egg
    ½ cup orange juice
    ¼ cup water
    ½ cup chopped nuts

OVEN 375°   I LOAF

In small mixing bowl, cover dried apricots with warm water and let stand 15 minutes. Drain; cut into pieces. In large mixing bowl, combine flour, sugar, baking powder, salt and soda. Add shortening, egg, orange juice and water. Mix until well blended. Stir in apricots and nuts. Mix well. Turn into 9x5-inch loaf pan which has been greased on the bottom only. Bake at 375° for 45 to 55 minutes, until toothpick inserted in center comes out clean. Remove from pan. Cool thoroughly before slicing.

*For use with Pillsbury's Best Self-Rising Flour, increase flour to 2¼ cups; omit baking powder, salt and soda.

HIGH ALTITUDE ADJUSTMENT — 5,200 FEET.
Reduce baking powder to I teaspoon. Line bottom of pan with greased, waxed paper.

Baking powder biscuits go Italiano with snappy green pepper, pimiento and Cheddar cheese. Serve with soup in about 40 minutes.

Chipper Cheese Biscuits

    2 cups Pillsbury's Best All Purpose Flour*
    3 teaspoons baking powder
    I teaspoon salt
    ⅓ cup shortening
    ⅔ cup shredded American or Cheddar cheese
    2 tablespoons finely chopped green pepper
    I tablespoon chopped pimiento
    ¾ cup milk

OVEN 450°   18 BISCUITS

In large mixer bowl, combine flour, baking powder and salt. Cut in shortening until particles are fine. Blend in cheese, green pepper and pimiento; mix well. Add milk; mix only until dry particles are moistened. Knead gently on floured surface 12 times. Roll to ½-inch thickness and cut into rounds with floured 2½-inch cutter. Place on ungreased cookie sheet. Bake at 450° for 12 to 15 minutes until golden brown. Serve hot.

*For use with Pillsbury's Best Self-Rising Flour, omit baking powder and salt.

A spicy delightful version of cornbread, jeweled with raisins throughout, and topped with a cinnamon crumble. Yum! An hour 'til serving time.

Spicy Raisin Cornbread

Cornbread

    1¼ cups Pillsbury's Best All Purpose Flour*
    ¾ cup cornmeal
    ¼ cup sugar
    3 teaspoons baking powder
    I teaspoon salt
    I teaspoon cinnamon
    ¼ teaspoon ginger
    ¼ teaspoon allspice
    I cup milk
    2 tablespoons shortening, melted
    I egg
    ½ cup raisins

Topping

    ½ cup sugar
    I teaspoon cinnamon
    I tablespoon butter or margarine

OVEN 400°   9-INCH COFFEE CAKE

Cornbread: In large mixing bowl, combine all ingredients; blend well. Pour into well-greased 9-inch square pan. Sprinkle Topping over batter. Bake at 400° for 20 to 25 minutes until golden brown. Serve warm.

Topping: Combine sugar and cinnamon; cut in butter until particles are fine.

Tip: 2 tablespoons cooking oil may be used for the melted shortening.

*For use with Pillsbury's Best Self-Rising Flour, decrease baking powder to 1½ teaspoons and omit salt.

HIGH ALTITUDE ADJUSTMENT — 5,200 FEET.
Reduce baking powder to I teaspoon.

Good any time of year, but really great for the fall festival. It takes about an hour and a half to make.

Pumpkin Tea Loaf

  2 cups Pillsbury's Best All Purpose Flour*
  I cup firmly packed brown sugar
  I teaspoon salt
  I teaspoon soda
  I teaspoon cinnamon
  ½ teaspoon nutmeg
  ¼ teaspoon ginger
  ½ cup shortening
  2 eggs
  I cup canned or cooked pumpkin
  ¼ cup light molasses
  ¼ cup milk
  I teaspoon vanilla
  I cup chopped nuts, if desired

OVEN 350°   I LOAF

In large mixer bowl, combine all ingredients except nuts. Beat 3 minutes at medium speed. Stir in nuts. Turn into 9x5-inch loaf pan, which has been greased on the bottom only. Bake at 350° for 60 to 70 minutes, until toothpick inserted in center comes out clean. Cool. If desired, frost with Orange Frosting, page 12.

*For use with Pillsbury's Best Self-Rising Flour, omit soda and salt.

HIGH ALTITUDE ADJUSTMENT — 5,200 FEET. Reduce soda to ¾ teaspoon. Line bottom of pans with greased, waxed paper. Bake at 375° for 60 to 70 minutes.

The hearty texture of limpa makes news in quick-bread muffins . . . in only thirty minutes. Flavored with caraway or orange peel.

Swedish Limpa Muffins

  I cup rye flour
  ¾ cup Pillsbury's Best All Purpose Flour*
  ¼ cup firmly packed brown sugar
  4 teaspoons baking powder
  ½ teaspoon salt
  I to 2 teaspoons caraway seed or grated orange peel
  I egg, slightly beaten
  ¾ cup milk
  ¼ cup cooking oil
  ¼ cup molasses

OVEN 400°   I2 MUFFINS

In large mixing bowl, combine all ingredients.

Mix only until dry ingredients are moistened. Fill well-greased muffin cups about half full. Bake at 400° for I5 to 20 minutes until golden brown. Serve hot.

*For use with Pillsbury's Best Self-Rising Flour, decrease baking powder to 1 teaspoon and omit salt.

HIGH ALTITUDE ADJUSTMENT — 5,200 FEET. Reduce baking powder to 2 teaspoons.

Swirled in the tastiest of quick breads is a mouthwatering caramel and nut mixture. Sticky and delicious, and ready pronto in about 45 minutes.

Buttery Caramel Quicks

  ⅓ cup butter or margarine
  ⅓ cup firmly packed brown sugar
  I tablespoon water
  2 cups Pillsbury's Best All Purpose Flour*
  ¼ cup sugar
  2½ teaspoons baking powder
  I teaspoon salt
  ⅔ cup milk
  ⅓ cup firmly packed brown sugar
  I teaspoon cinnamon
  ⅓ cup chopped pecans

OVEN 425°   I2 ROLLS

In 9-inch square pan, melt butter. Stir in ⅓ cup brown sugar and water. Set aside.

In large mixing bowl, combine flour, sugar, baking powder and salt. Add milk all at once, stirring just until dry ingredients are moistened. Turn out onto well-floured surface. Roll out to a I2x10-inch rectangle. Combine ⅓ cup brown sugar, cinnamon and pecans. Sprinkle over dough. Roll up starting with I2-inch side. Cut into I-inch slices; place cut-side down in prepared pan. Bake at 425° for I8 to 22 minutes until golden brown. Turn out immediately. Serve hot.

*For use with Pillsbury's Best Self-Rising Flour, omit baking powder and salt.

HIGH ALTITUDE ADJUSTMENT — 5,200 FEET. Reduce baking powder to I½ teaspoons.

Snacks

● Tasty morsels to soften the hunger pangs and snap up the party . . . that's one of the functions of snacks. Whether you want a light fan-fare for your dinner-to-come, a hearty midnight supper bread, or just after-school nibble-ons, you'll find some extraordinary ones in this Bake Off collection. The recipes are complete with special dips and sauces, as well as tips for preparing them so you can enjoy your own party. A snack tray that says fun and variety automatically marks you as a hostess with the mostes'.

A great blend of cheese and spices top this round snack bread. Allow 2 hours . . . then serve hot from the oven on your favorite wood tray. Let your guests slice their own! Tip gives a fix-ahead idea.

Cheese-Crusted Flat Bread

2½ to 3 cups Pillsbury's Best All Purpose
    Flour*
  1 tablespoon sugar
1½ teaspoons salt
  1 package active dry yeast
  1 cup milk
  2 tablespoons butter or margarine
  1 cup shredded Cheddar cheese

Topping
  ¼ cup butter or margarine, melted
  2 tablespoons chopped onion
  ½ teaspoon paprika
  ½ teaspoon oregano
  ¼ teaspoon celery seed
  ¼ teaspoon garlic salt

OVEN 375°   2 LOAVES

In large mixer bowl, combine 1 cup of flour, sugar, salt and dry yeast. In saucepan, heat milk and butter until milk is warm. (Butter does not need to melt.) Add warm milk to flour mixture. Blend at low speed until moistened; beat 3 minutes at medium speed. By hand, stir in remaining flour to form a stiff dough. Knead on floured surface until smooth and satiny, about 4 minutes. Place in greased bowl, turning to grease top. Cover; let rise in warm place until doubled in size, about 45 minutes. Prepare Topping.

Punch down dough; divide in half. Press each half into greased 9-inch round layer pan. Spread with Topping. Sprinkle with cheese; prick generously with a fork. Cover; let rise in warm place until light and doubled in size, about 30 minutes. Bake at 375° for 20 to 25 minutes until golden brown. Serve warm.

Topping: In small mixing bowl, combine all ingredients.

Tip: Prepare bread ahead, freeze or refrigerate. Reheat in foil at 350° for about 15 minutes until heated through.

*For use with Pillsbury's Best Self-Rising Flour, omit salt.

Cheesy potato pastry rounds made gay with paprika; great with this hot baked tuna dip. A distinctive canapé prepared in only half an hour.

Tuna-Tater Thins

1½ cups Pillsbury's Best All Purpose Flour*
  ½ cup Pillsbury Hungry Jack Mashed
      Potato Flakes
  ¼ cup grated Parmesan cheese
  ¼ teaspoon hot pepper sauce
  ½ cup butter or margarine, softened
  4 to 5 tablespoons cold water
      Paprika

Hot Tuna Dip
  1 package (8 oz.) cream cheese, softened
  1 can (6½ oz.) tuna, drained
  2 tablespoons chopped almonds
  1 tablespoon instant minced onion
  1 tablespoon horseradish
  ¼ teaspoon garlic salt
  ¼ teaspoon salt
      Dash pepper
  3 to 4 tablespoons milk

OVEN 375°   ABOUT 30 SNACKS

In large mixing bowl, combine flour, potato flakes, cheese and hot pepper sauce. Cut in butter until mixture is crumbly. Sprinkle water, a little at a time, over mixture, tossing and stirring lightly with a fork until dough is moist enough to hold together. Roll out on well-floured surface to ⅛-inch thickness. Cut into rounds with 2-inch cutter. Place on ungreased cookie sheets. Sprinkle with paprika. Bake at 375° for 12 to 15 minutes until golden brown. Serve with Hot Tuna Dip.

Hot Tuna Dip: In large mixing bowl, combine all ingredients until of dip consistency. Place in small baking dish. Garnish with additional almonds. Bake at 375° for about 10 minutes until hot throughout. (May take about 20 minutes if mixture is chilled.)

*For use with Pillsbury's Best Self-Rising Flour, omit salt.

A ready-made novel sandwich to serve hot and handsome. Meat-cheese-olive filling swirled in a crisp-crusted French bread. Make in two hours; freeze one for later.

French Boy Loaf

    4 to 4½ cups Pillsbury's Best All Purpose
        Flour*
    I tablespoon sugar
    1½ teaspoons salt
    I package active dry yeast
    1½ cups warm water
    2 tablespoons shortening
    2 tablespoons butter or margarine, melted
    2 teaspoons sesame seeds

Filling
    I can (12 oz.) finely chopped luncheon meat
    ¾ cup shredded Cheddar cheese
    ½ cup finely chopped walnuts
    ¼ cup thinly sliced stuffed green olives
    ¼ cup thinly sliced ripe olives

OVEN 400°   2 LOAVES

In large mixer bowl, combine 2 cups of flour, sugar, salt and dry yeast. Add warm water and shortening. Blend at low speed until moistened; beat 3 minutes at medium speed. By hand, stir in remaining flour to form a stiff dough. Prepare Filling.

Divide dough into two portions. Roll out each on a floured surface to a 12x9-inch rectangle. Brush with melted butter; spread with Filling to within ½ inch of edges. Starting with 12-inch side, roll up jelly-roll fashion, sealing edges and ends. Place seam-side down on greased cookie sheets. Make diagonal slashes about 2 inches apart on top of loaves. Brush with melted butter and sprinkle with sesame seeds. Let rise in warm place until light and doubled in size, I to 1½ hours. Bake at 400° for 30 to 35 minutes until golden brown. Serve hot.

Filling: In small mixing bowl, combine all ingredients; mix well.

Tips: Freeze one loaf to keep for "emergency" snacks.

Store leftover portions of loaf in refrigerator and reheat, wrapped in foil, in a 350° oven for about 20 minutes.

*For use with Pillsbury's Best Self-Rising Flour, omit salt.

A great meaty snack-bread . . . quick and easy, less than two hours a-making. The twisted loaves are sprinkled with caraway. Serve one, freeze one.

Corned Beef Rye Twist

    2 cups rye flour
    ½ cup Pillsbury Hungry Jack Mashed
        Potato Flakes
    2 tablespoons firmly packed brown sugar
    I tablespoon caraway seed
    3 teaspoons salt
    2 packages active dry yeast
    I cup warm water
    I can (II oz.) condensed Cheddar cheese
        soup
    2 tablespoons cooking oil
    I can (12 oz.) finely chopped corned beef
    3 to 3½ cups Pillsbury's Best All Purpose
        Flour*
    I teaspoon caraway seed

OVEN 375°   2 LOAVES

In large mixer bowl, combine rye flour, potato flakes, brown sugar, I tablespoon caraway seed, salt, dry yeast, warm water, Cheddar cheese soup, cooking oil and corned beef. Blend at low speed until moistened; beat 3 minutes at medium speed. By hand, stir in all purpose flour to form a stiff dough. Knead on floured surface until smooth and elastic, about 4 minutes. Divide dough into quarters. Shape each portion into a 10-inch strip. In well-greased 9x5-inch loaf pans, twist two strips together; seal ends. Cover; let rise in warm place until light and doubled in size, about 45 minutes. Brush with milk and sprinkle with I teaspoon caraway seed. Bake at 375° for 30 to 35 minutes. Remove from pans; cool on wire rack.

Tips: For leftover part of loaf, store in refrigerator and reheat in foil in 350° oven for about 20 minutes.

Freeze one loaf to use at a later time.

*For use with Pillsbury's Best Self-Rising Flour, omit salt.

A crusty delight! Easy, cheesy squares sprinkled with poppy or caraway seeds. Serve it oven-warm in about 3 hours.

Cheese Snack Bread

2½ cups Pillsbury's Best All Purpose Flour*
   I tablespoon sugar
   I teaspoon salt
   I package active dry yeast
   I cup milk
   2 tablespoons shortening
1½ teaspoons poppy or caraway seeds

Topping
2½ cups (½ lb.) shredded American cheese
   2 tablespoons chopped onion
   ¼ teaspoon salt
   ⅓ cup milk
   I egg

OVEN 425°   I5X10-INCH SNACK BREAD

In large mixing bowl, combine I cup of flour, sugar, salt and dry yeast. In saucepan, heat milk and shortening until milk is warm. (Shortening does not need to melt.) Add to flour mixture. Beat until smooth. Stir in remaining flour to form a stiff dough. Knead on floured surface until smooth and elastic, about 3 minutes. Place in greased bowl, turning to grease top. Cover; let rise in warm place until light and doubled in size, about one hour.

Punch down dough; press into greased I5x10-inch jelly roll pan. Spread with Topping; sprinkle with seeds. Cover; let rise in warm place until light and doubled in size, about 45 minutes. Bake at 425° for I5 to 20 minutes until golden brown. Serve warm, cut in squares.

Topping: In small mixing bowl, combine all ingredients; blend well.

*For use with Pillsbury's Best Self-Rising Flour, omit salt.

Bits of dried beef, enhanced with Parmesan cheese, make these snack strips distinctive. Easily made in thirty minutes, and you can do 'em ahead, too.

Dice O'Derv

   I package Pillsbury Pie Crust Mix
   ½ cup (1½ oz.) grated Parmesan cheese
   ¾ cup (2½ oz. jar) cut-up dried beef

OVEN 450°   ABOUT 72 SNACKS

Prepare pie crust mix as directed on package, adding cheese and dried beef to dry mix. Form into a ball; divide in half. Roll out each portion on floured surface to ⅛-inch thickness. Cut into 2½x1½-inch strips with pastry wheel or sharp knife. Place on ungreased cookie sheets. Bake at 450° for 5 to 7 minutes until golden brown. Serve warm or cold.

Tips: Snacks may be prepared ahead, wrapped tightly and stored in refrigerator or freezer until ready to bake.

For about 36 snacks, use half a package of pie crust mix, adding half the cheese and dried beef.

Four little loaves bake together for this bright idea snack bread. A light bread, colorfully polka-dotted with olive chunks and smacking subtly of dill. Two hours easy.

Olive Polka-Dot Bread

3¼ to 3¾ cups Pillsbury's Best All Purpose Flour*
   3 tablespoons sugar
   ½ teaspoon salt
   2 packages active dry yeast
   I packet dry dill dip mix
   I cup warm water
   I egg
   3 tablespoons butter or margarine
   ½ cup quartered ripe olives
   ¼ cup quartered stuffed green olives

OVEN 375°   I LOAF

In large mixer bowl, combine 2 cups of flour with remaining ingredients. Blend at low speed until moistened; beat 3 minutes at medium speed. By hand, stir in remaining flour to form a stiff dough. Cover; let rise in warm place until light and doubled in size, about 30 minutes.

Stir down dough; toss on floured surface until no longer sticky. Roll out to a I6x6-inch rectangle. Starting with I6-inch side, roll up jelly-roll fashion. Cut into four 4-inch rolls. Place crosswise, side by side, in greased 9x5-inch loaf pan. Cover; let rise in warm place until light and doubled in size, I5 to 30 minutes. Bake at 375° for 30 to 35 minutes until golden brown. Remove from pan immediately. Brush with butter.

*For use with Pillsbury's Best Self-Rising Flour, omit salt.

A super party snack: tiny meat balls wrapped in a rich curry and cheese pastry, served hot. And, they can be made ahead and chilled before baking.

Meat Balls A Go-Go

     2 cups shredded sharp Cheddar cheese
     ½ cup butter or margarine, softened
     1½ cups Pillsbury's Best All Purpose Flour*
     2 teaspoons curry powder
     ½ teaspoon salt
     ¼ teaspoon hot pepper sauce

Meat Balls
     ½ lb. lean ground beef
     ½ teaspoon salt
     ½ teaspoon instant minced onion
     ¼ teaspoon pepper

OVEN 425°   ABOUT 40 SNACKS

In large mixing bowl, combine cheese and butter. Add flour, curry powder, salt and hot pepper sauce. Mix until well blended. (Mixture will be dry and crumbly.) With hands, work mixture until it forms a ball. Pinch off slight tablespoonfuls of dough; flatten in palm of hand. Wrap around tiny meat balls. Place on ungreased cookie sheets. Bake at 425° for 15 to 17 minutes until golden brown. Serve hot.

Meat Balls: In small mixing bowl, combine all ingredients and mix well. Form into tiny meat balls.

Tip: Snacks may be prepared in advance and stored in the refrigerator or freezer until ready to bake.

*For use with Pillsbury's Best Self-Rising Flour, omit salt in cheese mixture.

Capture stuffed olives in this cheesy wrap-around, and you've captured your snack crowd for sure. Make ahead . . . and then bake just as guests arrive.

Olive Cheese Nuggets

     1 cup (4 oz.) shredded Cheddar cheese
     ¼ cup butter or margarine, softened
     ½ teaspoon paprika
     ⅛ teaspoon salt
     ¾ cup Pillsbury's Best All Purpose Flour*
     24 medium-sized stuffed green olives

OVEN 400°   24 SNACKS

In mixing bowl, combine cheese, butter, paprika and salt; blend well. Add flour, mixing well to form a dough. Shape rounded teaspoonfuls of dough around olives to cover completely. Place on ungreased cookie sheet. Bake at 400° for 12 to 15 minutes until golden brown. Serve hot or cold.

Tip: To prepare ahead, shape nuggets, wrap tightly and refrigerate. Place on cookie sheet and bake just before serving.

*For use with Pillsbury's Best Self-Rising Flour, omit salt.

Dainty yellow puff balls of minced clam served hot to dip in a chilly cocktail sauce. Very fancy fare for only forty-five minutes' time.

Beach Balls

     1 can (7½ or 8 oz.) minced clams
     ½ cup butter or margarine
     ½ teaspoon poultry seasoning
     ¼ teaspoon salt
     1 cup Pillsbury's Best All Purpose Flour*
     4 eggs

Cocktail Sauce
     1½ cups catsup
     ¼ cup finely chopped celery
     2 teaspoons cream-style horseradish
     2 teaspoons Worcestershire sauce
     2 teaspoons lemon juice
     ½ teaspoon onion salt
        Dash hot pepper sauce

OVEN 400°   ABOUT 48 SNACKS

Drain clams; reserve liquid. Add water to liquid to make 1 cup. In saucepan, heat liquid, butter, poultry seasoning and salt to boiling. Add flour all at once; cook and stir over medium heat until mixture leaves sides of pan and forms a stiff ball. Remove from heat. Add eggs, one at a time, beating well after each addition. Stir in clams. Drop by teaspoons onto ungreased cookie sheets. Bake at 400° for 18 to 20 minutes until golden brown. Serve warm with Cocktail Sauce.

Cocktail Sauce: In small mixing bowl, combine all ingredients. Chill.

Tip: Make ahead, freeze or refrigerate; then reheat on cookie sheets in 350° oven for about 10 minutes.

*For use with Pillsbury's Best Self-Rising Flour, omit salt.

Cheesy meat-topped snack bread . . . great hot from the oven in only 45 minutes. Cut into any size or shape and presto—an interesting, colorful snack tray. Follow tip for an easy make-ahead.

Deviled Snack Bread

2 to 2½ cups Pillsbury's Best All Purpose Flour*
2 tablespoons sugar
1 teaspoon salt
¼ teaspoon soda
1 package active dry yeast
½ cup dairy sour cream
¼ cup water
1 egg
2 tablespoons cooking oil

Topping

1 can (12 oz.) luncheon meat, finely chopped
1 cup shredded Cheddar cheese
⅓ cup chopped onion
⅓ cup chopped green pepper
3 tablespoons catsup
1 tablespoon prepared mustard

OVEN 350°   12 TO 15 SERVINGS

In large mixer bowl, combine 1 cup of flour, sugar, salt, soda and dry yeast. In saucepan, heat sour cream and water until warm. Add warm liquid, egg and cooking oil to dry ingredients. Blend at low speed until dry ingredients are moistened; beat 3 minutes at medium speed. By hand, stir in remaining flour to form a stiff dough.

Prepare Topping. Roll out or press dough to a 15x10-inch rectangle on a well-greased cookie sheet. Spread Topping on dough to within ½-inch of edges. Bake at 350° for 25 to 30 minutes until golden brown. Serve hot.

Topping: In large mixing bowl, combine all ingredients.

Tips: Bake Snack Bread ahead, cover and refrigerate. Then, wrap in foil and heat in a 350° oven for about 15 minutes.

For extra quick snacks, put a tablespoon of Topping in center of Pillsbury Refrigerated Quick Crescent Dinner Rolls (use 2 cans of rolls; ½ recipe of Topping). Bake as directed on package.

*For use with Pillsbury's Best Self-Rising Flour, omit salt and soda.

MENU
"After The Theatre" Party
Deviled Snack Bread
Tuna-Tater Thins (Page 126)
Ham Sensations (Page 138)
Beverage

Tiny cheese-and-sausage balls served hot, accompanied by a piquant pizza sauce for snappy dipping. An hour to prepare, or do 'em in advance.

Pizza Dippers

½ pound pork sausage
2 cups Pillsbury's Best All Purpose Flour*
¼ cup grated Parmesan cheese
1 teaspoon salt
⅔ cup shortening
6 to 7 tablespoons cold water

Pizza Sauce

1 cup (8 oz. can) tomato sauce
2 tablespoons grated Parmesan cheese
1 tablespoon cooking oil
¼ teaspoon ground oregano
¼ teaspoon garlic salt

OVEN 450°   ABOUT 40 SNACKS

In skillet, crumble and brown sausage. Drain and set aside. In large mixing bowl, combine flour, Parmesan cheese and salt. With pastry blender, cut in shortening until particles are fine. Stir in sausage. Add water, stirring with a fork until a dough forms. Shape into balls, 1 inch in diameter. Place on ungreased cookie sheets. Bake at 450° for 12 to 15 minutes until lightly browned. Serve hot, dipped in Pizza Sauce.

Pizza Sauce: In saucepan, combine all ingredients. Heat to boiling; simmer 5 minutes.

Tips: Cover and refrigerate balls up to 3 hours before baking.

Or, make early and then reheat by placing on cookie sheets in 300° oven for 10 minutes.

*For use with Pillsbury's Best Self-Rising Flour, omit salt.

Pizza Dippers

Cheese Secrets

Tidbit Toppers

Golden Cheesies

131

Rolls of flaky, golden pastry with bubbly cheese peeking through. Make early; then bake just before serving — fun and tasty!

Golden Cheesies

    1 package Pillsbury Pie Crust Mix
    2 tablespoons cooking sherry
1½ cups shredded Cheddar cheese
    Paprika

OVEN 400°   ABOUT 24 SNACKS

Prepare pie crust mix as directed on package, using 2 tablespoons cooking sherry in place of part of water. Divide in half. Roll out each portion on floured surface to a 12x4-inch rectangle. Sprinkle with cheese. Fold 12-inch edges over center, sealing edges and ends. Place, seam-side down, on ungreased cookie sheet. Using sharp knife, cut halfway through rolls at 1-inch intervals. Sprinkle with paprika. Bake at 400° for 15 to 20 minutes until golden brown. Serve hot.

Tip: Make Golden Cheesies ahead, cover and refrigerate; bake just before serving.

Bite-size puffs in only 30 minutes. Soft, cheesy center . . . great warm or cold. Tip gives a sherry flavor variation.

Cheese Secrets

    ½ cup water
    ¼ cup butter
    ¼ teaspoon salt
    ½ cup Pillsbury's Best All Purpose Flour*
    2 eggs
    4 ounces cream cheese, softened
    1 jar (5 oz.) pasteurized process sharp American cheese spread, softened

OVEN 400°   48 PUFFS

In saucepan, combine water, butter and salt. Heat to boiling. Add flour all at once, stirring constantly until mixture forms a ball and leaves sides of pan. Remove from heat. Blend in eggs, one at a time, beating vigorously after each until mixture is smooth and glossy. Stir in softened cheeses until well blended. Drop dough by teaspoons onto well-greased cookie sheets. Bake at 400° for 15 to 20 minutes until golden brown. Remove from cookie sheets immediately. Serve warm or cold.

Tips: Fix ahead and reheat on ungreased cookie sheets in 350° oven for 10 minutes. Serve hot.

Stir in 2 tablespoons cooking sherry with flour. Prepare as directed above. Serve hot.

*For use with Pillsbury's Best Self-Rising Flour, omit salt.

Rich, cheesy dough-drops that can be topped with plain or exotic tidbits to make a varied and colorful appetizer tray as wild as your imagination. Give yourself only thirty minutes.

Tidbit Toppers

    2 cups Pillsbury's Best All Purpose Flour*
    3 teaspoons baking powder
    1 teaspoon salt
    1 packet (1⅜ oz.) dry cheese sauce mix or 1 cup shredded Cheddar cheese
    1 cup milk
    ⅓ cup butter or margarine, melted

Toppers
    Small smoked sausage links, cut into ½-inch pieces
    Button mushrooms
    Stuffed green or pitted ripe olives
    Crumbled bacon or bacon-flavored bits
    Sharp Cheddar cheese, cut into ½-inch cubes
    Caraway seed
    Cocktail onions

OVEN 400°   30 TO 36 SNACKS

In large mixing bowl, combine flour, baking powder, salt, cheese sauce mix, milk and butter. Drop dough by teaspoons onto ungreased cookie sheets. Make an indentation in center of each; insert a "topper". Bake at 400° for 10 to 12 minutes until light brown. Serve hot.

*For use with Pillsbury's Best Self-Rising Flour, omit baking powder and salt.

A delightful mixture of sweet and piquant! Pizza-shaped snacks in only forty-five minutes that feature sweet relish in the crust and cheesy-sour cream topped corned beef.

Cheeza Corned Beef

   2 cups Pillsbury's Best All Purpose Flour*
   2 teaspoons baking powder
   ⅔ cup pickle relish mayonnaise (sandwich spread)
   ⅓ cup milk
   1 can (12 oz.) corned beef
   1 cup shredded Cheddar cheese
   ¾ cup dairy sour cream
   ½ teaspoon dry mustard

OVEN 425°   14-INCH PIZZA

In large mixing bowl, combine flour and baking powder. Add pickle relish, mayonnaise and milk. Stir until dough clings together in a ball. With floured fingers, press into bottom of ungreased 14-inch pizza pan. Break up corned beef; sprinkle over crust. In small mixing bowl, combine cheese, sour cream and dry mustard; drop by spoonfuls over corned beef; spread to cover. Bake at 425° for 20 to 25 minutes until golden brown. Serve hot.

Tip: If desired, a 12-inch pizza pan or a 13x9-inch pan may be used.

*For use with Pillsbury's Best Self-Rising Flour, add 2 tablespoons additional flour and omit baking powder.

Hot little rounds that will make complimentary conversation, with their sweet-sour note of chutney 'n ham. Ready to serve in less than forty-five minutes or make them ahead.

Ham Chutney Canapés

    1 can Pillsbury Refrigerated Tender-flake Biscuits
    1 cup (½ lb.) ground cooked ham
    ½ cup shredded Cheddar cheese
    ¼ cup finely chopped chutney or sweet gherkin pickles
    ¼ cup chopped parsley
    ¼ cup light cream
    1 teaspoon grated onion

OVEN 400°   36 CANAPES

Separate each biscuit into 3 thin biscuit wafers. Place on ungreased cookie sheets. Bake at 400° for 8 to 10 minutes until golden brown. In small mixing bowl, combine remaining ingredients; mix well. Place teaspoonfuls of ham mixture on each biscuit wafer. Bake at 400° for 10 to 12 minutes until ham mixture is hot. Serve hot.

<u>Tip:</u> To make ahead, bake biscuits and prepare ham filling. Then, assemble and bake just before serving.

Don't have to be an Italian to love this super supper loaf! So easy with refrigerated pizza dough. Fried potatoes and onions combine with Cheddar cheese for the filling. What a prize in only 45 minutes!

Italian Supper Loaf

    ⅓ cup cooking oil
    2 cups (2 medium) diced potato
    ¾ cup (1 medium) thinly sliced onion
    1 package Pillsbury Refrigerated Seasoned Pizza Dough and Pizza Sauce
    2 tablespoons flour
    ½ teaspoon salt
    ½ cup shredded Cheddar cheese
    3 tablespoons grated Parmesan cheese

OVEN 400°   1 LOAF

In medium skillet, cook potatoes in cooking oil over medium heat, about 10 minutes, turning often. Add sliced onion; continue cooking for 10 minutes until tender. Remove from heat. Combine pizza sauce, flour and salt. Add to potatoes and onions; mix well. Cool completely.

Unroll pizza dough on ungreased cookie sheet, placing seasoned side up. Spread potato filling over dough to within 1 inch of edges. Sprinkle with shredded Cheddar cheese and Parmesan cheese. Roll up, jelly-roll fashion, starting with longest side. Seal edge and ends. Be sure roll is seam-side down on cookie sheet. Prick top with fork; brush with milk. Bake at 400° for 10 to 15 minutes until golden brown. Serve warm, cut in slices.

<u>Tip:</u> For a main dish treat, sprinkle ½ cup crumbled crisp bacon over cheese.

Ahoy mates! Here's a snack to please any landlubber. And it can be made ahead or reheated for your pleasure.

Shrimp Bubbles

    ½ cup butter or margarine, softened
    1 package (8 oz.) cream cheese
    1 cup Pillsbury's Best All Purpose or Self-Rising Flour
    3 to 4 tablespoons light cream or milk

<u>*Shrimp Filling*</u>
    1 can (4½ oz.) tiny shrimp, drained and flaked
    ¼ cup salad dressing or mayonnaise
    1 teaspoon instant minced onion
    ½ teaspoon monosodium glutamate

OVEN 375°   ABOUT 60 SNACKS

In large mixing bowl, cut butter and cream cheese into flour until well blended and crumbly. Add cream, stirring with a fork until a dough forms. Toss on well-floured cloth covered surface until no longer sticky. Divide in half; shape into balls. Roll out each on floured cloth surface to ⅛-inch thickness. Cut into rounds with 2-inch cutter. Place on ungreased cookie sheets. Place a scant half teaspoonful of Shrimp Filling in center of each round. Fold in half; seal edges. Bake at 375° for 15 to 18 minutes until light golden brown. Serve hot with favorite seafood cocktail sauce.

<u>Shrimp Filling:</u> In mixing bowl, combine all ingredients. Blend well.

<u>Tips:</u> Cover and refrigerate snacks up to 3 hours before baking.

Or, make early and then reheat by placing on cookie sheet in 300° oven for 8 to 10 minutes.

Hot puffs of curried tuna made special with green pepper and cheese. A dipper's delight, and they can be made ahead!

Tuna Teasers

  1½ cups Pillsbury's Best All Purpose Flour*
   1 teaspoon baking powder
  ½ teaspoon onion salt
  ½ teaspoon curry powder
   Dash cayenne pepper
  ½ cup butter or margarine, softened
   3 to 4 tablespoons milk
   1 can (6½ oz.) tuna, drained
   1 cup shredded Cheddar cheese
   1 tablespoon finely minced green pepper

OVEN 450°   ABOUT 36 SNACKS

In large mixing bowl, combine flour, baking powder, onion salt, curry powder and cayenne pepper. Cut in butter until mixture is crumbly. Add milk, stirring until mixture holds together. Add tuna, cheese and green pepper, stirring to blend. Shape into balls; place on greased cookie sheet. Bake at 450° for 10 to 12 minutes until golden brown. Serve hot with cocktail sauce, if desired.

Tip: Tuna Teasers may be shaped, covered and stored in the refrigerator or freezer; then, place on cookie sheets and bake just before serving.

*For use with Pillsbury's Best Self-Rising Flour, omit baking powder.

Satisfy the snackers in your family with this jiffy new treat. Pretzel-thin snacks full of rich, cheese tang.

Cheese Nibblers

  ⅔ cup firmly packed Pillsbury Pie Crust Mix
   1 cup (4 oz. pkg.) shredded Cheddar cheese
   2 tablespoons butter or margarine, melted
   2 tablespoons cold water

OVEN 450°   ABOUT 60 SNACKS

In small mixing bowl, combine pie crust mix and cheese. Combine butter and water; add to dry ingredients. Stir with fork until dough forms. Shape into pencil-thin sticks, using scant teaspoonful of dough for each. Place on ungreased cookie sheets. Bake at 450° for 6 to 8 minutes until golden brown. Serve warm.

Tip: Make early, cover and refrigerate. Bake just before serving.

Pigs in a blanket, cocktail style. Little sausages wrapped in refrigerated crescent dough. Easy made in 20 minutes, or prepare ahead.

Sausage Snacks

   1 can Pillsbury Refrigerated Quick Crescent
    Dinner Rolls
  ⅓ cup grated Parmesan cheese
  16 cocktail or Vienna sausages
    Milk
    Poppy seeds or sesame seeds

OVEN 375°   16 SNACKS

Unroll crescent dough; separate into 8 triangles. Cut each lengthwise to make 16 triangles. Sprinkle each with about 1 teaspoon Parmesan cheese. Place 1 cocktail wiener on wide end of triangle and roll up. Dip in milk; place on ungreased cookie sheet. Sprinkle with poppy seeds or sesame seeds. Bake at 375° for 10 to 12 minutes until golden brown. Serve with catsup or mustard.

Tip: These can be prepared up to 4 hours in advance. Place unbaked snacks on cookie sheet; cover tightly with plastic wrap and refrigerate. Bake at 375° for 12 to 15 minutes until golden brown.

Crispy-quick appetizers from pie crust mix that you make in less than half an hour! Or, prepare early and bake just before serving.

Cheese Caraway Nips

   1 package Pillsbury Pie Crust Mix or Sticks
   2 teaspoons dry mustard
   2 teaspoons caraway seed
  ½ cup shredded Cheddar cheese

OVEN 450°   ABOUT 60 SNACKS

Prepare pie crust mix as directed on package for one-crust pie, adding dry mustard, caraway seed and cheese to dry mix. Form into 2 balls. Roll out each on floured surface to 10x9-inch rectangle. Cut into 3x1-inch strips. Place on ungreased cookie sheets. Bake at 450° for 6 to 9 minutes until golden brown.

Tips: ½ cup finely chopped caraway cheese may be substituted for the Cheddar cheese and caraway seed.

Prepare early, cover and refrigerate. Bake just before serving.

A meaty loaf, with colorful chips of salami right in the dough . . . spun with a hint of garlic. A great snack or a meal with a bowl of soup in just four hours.

Soup and Sandwich Bread

2½ to 3 cups Pillsbury's Best All Purpose
    Flour*
  2 tablespoons sugar
1½ teaspoons salt
  2 packages active dry yeast
  ¼ cup instant minced onion
  ¼ teaspoon garlic salt
    I cup warm water
    I tablespoon cooking oil
    I cup finely chopped salami

OVEN 375°   I LOAF

In large mixer bowl, combine I cup of flour

with remaining ingredients except salami. Blend at low speed until moistened; beat 3 minutes at medium speed. By hand, stir in salami and remaining flour to form a stiff dough. Knead on floured surface until smooth and satiny, 3 to 5 minutes. Place in greased bowl, turning to grease top. Cover; let rise in warm place until light and doubled in size, 1 to 1½ hours.

Punch down dough; shape into a loaf (see page 22). Place seam-side down, in well-greased 9x5-inch loaf pan. Cover; let rise in warm place until light and doubled in size, about 1 hour. Bake at 375° for 35 to 40 minutes until golden brown. Brush with butter; remove from pan. Cool.

*For use with Pillsbury's Best Self-Rising Flour, omit salt.

It's no trick to make, though. This savory snack bread goes together fast, is done in two hours. Four savory loaves that make terrific toast.

Double Trick Cheese Bread

3½ to 3¾ cups Pillsbury's Best All Purpose
    or Self-Rising Flour
2 packages active dry yeast
1 packet dry garlic salad dressing mix
1 can (11 oz.) condensed Cheddar cheese
    soup
½ cup warm water

OVEN 400°   4 SMALL LOAVES

In large mixer bowl, combine 1½ cups of flour with remaining ingredients. Blend at low speed until dry ingredients are moistened; beat 3 minutes at medium speed. By hand, stir in remaining flour to form a stiff dough. Knead on floured surface until smooth and elastic, about 5 minutes. Place in greased bowl, turning to grease top. Cover; let rise in warm place until light and doubled in size, about 30 minutes.

Punch down dough. Shape into four 10-inch long loaves; place on greased cookie sheets. Cover; let rise in warm place until light and doubled in size, about 30 minutes. Bake at 400° for 30 to 35 minutes until golden brown. Remove from cookie sheets immediately. Brush with butter. Cool.

Tip: If desired, slice and toast in 250° oven for 10 minutes.

Crispy finger-food for hors d'oeuvres or snacks. Zesty sesame and onion rounds that can be made ahead.

Savory Snacks

2 cups Pillsbury's Best All Purpose Flour*
3 teaspoons baking powder
1 teaspoon salt
½ cup shortening
⅔ cup milk
    Butter or margarine, softened
½ cup finely chopped onion
2 tablespoons sesame seeds

OVEN 450°   80 SNACKS

In large mixing bowl, combine flour, baking powder and salt. Cut in shortening until particles are fine. Add milk all at once, stirring just until all dry particles are moistened.

Divide dough in half. Roll out each half on floured surface to a 20x12-inch rectangle. Brush with butter and sprinkle each with half of the chopped onion and sesame seeds. Roll up each starting with 20-inch edge. Seal edge well. Cut into ½-inch slices. Place on greased cookie sheets; flatten slightly. Bake at 450° for 10 to 12 minutes until golden brown. Serve hot.

Tips: Make early and then reheat by placing on cookie sheet in 300° oven for 10 minutes.

Or, cover and refrigerate unsliced rolls up to 3 hours before slicing and baking.

For small groups, use half a recipe.

*For use with Pillsbury's Best Self-Rising Flour, omit baking powder and salt.

HIGH ALTITUDE ADJUSTMENT — 5,200 FEET. Reduce baking powder to 1½ teaspoons.

Tiny roll-ups of Cheddar cheese dough filled with ham and french fried onion rings. Serve hot for toothpicks or fingers in thirty to forty-five minutes.

Ham Sensations

1½ cups Pillsbury's Best All Purpose or
    Self-Rising Flour
1 cup (4 oz. package) shredded Cheddar
    cheese
¼ teaspoon cayenne pepper
½ cup butter or margarine, softened
¼ cup cold water
8 thin slices boiled ham
1 can (3½ oz.) french fried onions,
    crumbled

OVEN 450°   40 SNACKS

In large mixer bowl, combine flour, cheese, cayenne pepper and butter. Gradually add water, mixing at low speed of mixer until a dough forms. Knead on floured surface 12 times.

Divide dough in half. Roll out each on floured surface to a 14x10-inch rectangle. Cut each into four 7x5-inch rectangles. Place a slice of ham on each rectangle; sprinkle with onions. Starting with 5-inch side, roll up; seal edge. Place, seam-side down, on greased cookie sheet. Bake at 450° for 10 to 12 minutes until golden brown. Remove from cookie sheet. Cut each roll into 5 slices. Serve hot.

Tip: Prepare early, cover and refrigerate. Bake just before serving.

Crisp, crumbled bacon combines with crispy rice cereal and cheese. Results? A crunchy hot snack that will make 'em smack their lips and ask for more! Takes only thirty minutes to bring them sizzling from the oven.

Snackeroons

    1 cup shredded Cheddar cheese
    ¾ cup Pillsbury's Best All Purpose or
        Self-Rising Flour
    ¾ cup rice crispy cereal, slightly crushed
    ½ cup chopped walnuts
    ½ teaspoon garlic salt
    6 slices crisp, crumbled bacon
    2 tablespoons bacon drippings or
        cooking oil
    3 tablespoons cooking sherry or water

OVEN 375°   ABOUT 36 SNACKS

In large mixing bowl, mix all ingredients until crumbly and thoroughly mixed. Form rounded teaspoonfuls into balls. Place on greased cookie sheets. Bake at 375° for 10 to 12 minutes until golden brown. Remove from cookie sheets immediately. Serve warm.

Tip: To make ahead, shape into balls, place in plastic bag and refrigerate. Place on cookie sheets and bake just before serving.

Fun-shaped puffs of flaky pastry, layered with a tangy bleu cheese-flavored filling. They'll melt in your mouth in thirty to forty-five minutes.

Bleu Cheese Puffs

    1 packet bleu cheese salad dressing mix
    2 teaspoons instant minced onion
    2 tablespoons butter or margarine, softened
    1 egg
    1 package (8 oz.) cream cheese
    2 cups Pillsbury's Best All Purpose Flour*
    1 teaspoon salt
    ¾ cup shortening
    5 to 6 tablespoons water
    Milk
    Sesame seeds

OVEN 425°   ABOUT 36 SNACKS

In small mixer bowl, combine salad dressing mix, minced onion, butter, egg and cream cheese. Blend 2 minutes at low speed. Set aside.

In small mixing bowl, combine flour and salt.

With pastry blender, cut in shortening until particles are fine. Add water, stirring with a fork until dough forms. Roll out on floured surface to a 20x14-inch rectangle. Cut into two 10x14-inch rectangles. Spread filling over one rectangle. Top with other rectangle of pastry. Using a cutter or knife, cut into various shapes. Place on ungreased cookie sheets. Brush with milk; sprinkle with sesame seeds. Bake at 425° for 12 to 15 minutes until lightly browned. Serve hot.

Tip: Make early, cover and refrigerate. Bake just before serving.

*For use with Pillsbury's Best Self-Rising Flour, omit salt.

Need a great snack for a party tonight? Take a half hour — the result is these tasty deviled ham bites. Serve 'em hot from the oven. Take a glance at the tip for easy make-aheads.

Ham 'N Tater Pom Poms

    ½ cup water
    ⅓ cup butter or margarine
    ½ teaspoon salt
    ⅛ teaspoon pepper
    1 cup Pillsbury Hungry Jack Mashed
        Potato Flakes
    1 cup Pillsbury's Best All Purpose Flour*
    2 teaspoons baking powder
    2 teaspoons instant minced onion
    1 teaspoon parsley flakes
    1 egg
    2 cans (4½ oz. each) luncheon meat
        spread or deviled ham
    Parmesan cheese

OVEN 400°   ABOUT 48 SNACKS

In saucepan, heat water, butter, salt and pepper to boiling. Remove from heat. Add potato flakes; whip lightly with fork. Add remaining ingredients; blend well. Drop dough by slightly rounded teaspoons onto ungreased cookie sheets. Sprinkle with Parmesan cheese. Bake at 400° for 12 to 15 minutes until golden brown. Serve warm.

Tip: Make ahead and refrigerate. Reheat by placing on cookie sheets in 350° oven for about 10 minutes.

*For use with Pillsbury's Best Self-Rising Flour, omit salt and baking powder.

Index

a

Almond
  Almond Frosting or Glaze . . . 12
  Almond Icing . . . 87
  Almond Marmalettes . . . 59
  Almond Rolls . . . 90
  Crunchy Cream-Filled
    Kuchen . . . 77
Aloha Banana Bread . . . 110
Ann Pillsbury Letter . . . 2
Apple
  Apple Country
    Coffee Cake . . . 68
  Pennsylvania
    Applesauce Bread . . . 114
  Peppy Apple-Cheese
    Bread . . . 108
  Raisin Apple Pair . . . 68
  Spicy Apple
    Crunch Cake . . . 106
Apricot
  Apricot Dandies . . . 94
  Holiday Treat . . . 123
  Nutty Apricot
    Snack Loaf . . . 122
  Sunny-Side-Up Rolls . . . 96
  Swedish Ripple
    Coffee Cake . . . 79

b

Bacon
  Snackeroons . . . 139
  Southern Bacon
    Brunchers . . . 114
Banana
  Aloha Banana Bread . . . 110
  Banana Luncheon Bread . . . 111
  Little Miss Muffins . . . 119
Barbecue Buns, Smoky . . . 50
Barbecue Twists . . . 53
Basics . . . 4
Batter Breads
  Almond Marmalettes . . . 59
  Carioca Coffee Cake . . . 56
  Dilly Casserole Bread . . . 56
  Easy Cheese Buns . . . 61
  Golden Cake Bread . . . 61

Half-Time Spoon Rolls . . . 62
  Honey Twin Rolls . . . 60
  No-Knead Holiday Bread . . . 58
  Raised Holiday Muffins . . . 62
  Savory Spoon Buns . . . 61
  Sugar Mountain Loaf . . . 60
  Tato-Flake Cheese Buns . . . 59
  Two-Way Coffee Bread . . . 58
Batter Breads Chapter . . . 54-64
Beach Balls . . . 129
Beauty Bow Coffee Cakes . . . 71
Biscuits
  Buttery Caramel Quicks . . . 123
  Chipper Cheese Biscuits . . . 122
  Onion Patch Pudding . . . 117
Bit O'Rye Breadsticks . . . 53
Bleu Cheese Puffs . . . 139
Blind Date Surprise Rolls . . . 96
Blueberry Brunch Loaf . . . 104
Bow Knots . . . 41
Bran
  Caraway Bran Bread . . . 27
  Country Garden
    Casserole Bread . . . 36
  Date-Rich Bran Bread . . . 110
  Prune Bran Loaf . . . 35
Brandy Frosting or Glaze . . . 12
Breadsticks
  Bit O'Rye Breadsticks . . . 53
  Herb Stickles . . . 52
Brioche, Flaky Butter . . . 48
Brown Breads
  Date-Rich Bran Bread . . . 110
  Graham Cracker
    Brown Bread . . . 109
  Merry Mince Brown Bread . . . 113
Butter Crispies . . . 99
Butter-Flake Rolls . . . 43
Butter-Nut Swirls . . . 88
Butter or Margarine,
    All About . . . 6
Buttercrust Flake-Aparts . . . 45
Butterflake Herb Loaf . . . 34
Butterflier "8's" . . . 83
Butterscotch Crescents,
    Double . . . 86
Buttery Caramel Quicks . . . 123

c

Can-Pan Fruit Bread . . . 29
Can Sizes . . . 11
Candied Fruit
  Can-Pan Fruit Bread . . . 29
  No-Knead Holiday Bread . . . 58
  Raised Holiday Muffins . . . 62
Caramel Rolls,
    Whole Wheat . . . 85
Caraway Bran Bread . . . 27
Caraway Nips, Cheese . . . 135
Carioca Coffee Cake . . . 56
Cheese
  Bleu Cheese Puffs . . . 139
  Cheese Caraway Nips . . . 135
  Cheese-Crusted
    Flat Bread . . . 126
  Cheese 'N Honey
    Topping . . . 15
  Cheese Nibblers . . . 135
  Cheese Popover Puffs . . . 118
  Cheese Roll Loaf . . . 37
  Cheese Secrets . . . 132
  Cheese Snack Bread . . . 128
  Cheeza Corned Beef . . . 133
  Chipper Cheese Biscuits . . . 122
  Chunk O'Cheese Bread . . . 37
  Clover Cheese Rolls . . . 46
  Corned Beef Rye Twist . . . 127
  Deviled Snack Bread . . . 130
  Double Trick
    Cheese Bread . . . 138
  Easy Cheesy Buns . . . 61
  French Boy Loaf . . . 127
  Garlic Cheese Toast . . . 28
  Golden Cheesies . . . 132
  Ham Sensations . . . 138
  Meat Balls A Go-Go . . . 129
  Olive Cheese Nuggets . . . 129
  Peppy Apple-Cheese
    Bread . . . 114
  Snackeroons . . . 139
  Tato-Flake Cheese Buns . . . 59
  Tidbit Toppers . . . 132
  Tuna Teasers . . . 135

Cherry
    Cherry Cheese Spread . . . 15
    Cherry Ring . . . 67
    European Coffee Cake . . . 79
Chipper Cheese Biscuits . . . 122
Chocolate Frosting
    or Glaze . . . 12
Chunk O'Cheese Bread . . . 37
Cinnamon
    Butter Crispies . . . 99
    Cinnamince Cider Buns . . . 95
    Cinnamon Crunch
      Coffee Cake . . . 112
    Cinnamon Nut Crisps . . . 98
    Cinnamon Pine-Rolls . . . 93
    Cinnamon Swirl
      Orange Loaf . . . 80
    Cinnamon Swirl
      Doughnuts . . . 100
    Coffee-Time
      Cinnamon Rolls . . . 83
    Frosty Cinnamon Twisters . . . 84
    Maple-Nut
      Cinnamon Rolls . . . 82
    Pineapple Supreme Rolls . . . 91
    Sweet Petals . . . 66
    Sweetheart Coffee Cake . . . 78
    Sunny-Side-Up Rolls . . . 96
    Topsy-Turvy Coffee Ring . . . 77
Clover Cheese Rolls . . . 46
Cloverleaf Rolls . . . 41
Cloverleaf Rolls, Quick . . . 41
Cocktail Sauce . . . 129
Coconut Butter Pastries . . . 92
Coffee Cakes, Quick
    Cinnamon Crunch
      Coffee Cake . . . 112
    Cranberry Crisscross
      Coffee Cake . . . 112
    Honey Ambrosia
      Coffee Cake . . . 113
    Jiffy Mince Coffee Ring . . . 107
    Kwik Peach Kuchen . . . 115
    Mandarin Coffee Cake . . . 112
    Peanut Butter
      Brunch Cake . . . 113
    Pecan Sunrise Bread . . . 107
    Royal Danish Kuchen . . . 107

    Spicy Apple Crunch Cake . . . 106
    Spicy Raisin Cornbread . . . 122
Coffee Cakes, Yeast
    Almond Marmalettes . . . 59
    Apple Country
      Coffee Cake . . . 68
    Beauty Bow Coffee Cakes . . . 71
    Carioca Coffee Cake . . . 56
    Cherry Ring . . . 67
    European Coffee Cake . . . 79
    Frosty Cinnamon Twisters . . . 84
    Hawaiian Coffee Ring . . . 76
    Honey Fingers . . . 85
    Lemon Twist Treat . . . 72
    Maple Butter Twists . . . 67
    Marmalade Twist . . . 70
    Merry-Go-Round
      Coffee Cake . . . 66
    Orange Blossom
      Coffee Cake . . . 74
    Orange Butter
      Coffee Cake . . . 74
    Peach Flip . . . 70
    Pineapple Raisin Tea Ring . . . 75
    Raisin Apple Pair . . . 68
    Rich Danish Coffee Cake . . . 76
    Snow Ring . . . 80
    Sugar Mountain Loaf . . . 60
    Sunflower Coffee Cake . . . 75
    Swedish Ripple
      Coffee Cake . . . 79
    Sweet Petals . . . 66
    Sweetheart Coffee Cake . . . 78
    Topsy-Turvy Coffee Ring . . . 77
    Two-Way Coffee Bread . . . 58
Coffee Cream Cheese Spread . . . 15
Coffee Frosting or Glaze . . . 12
Coffee-Time
    Cinnamon Rolls . . . 83
Coffee-Time Doughnuts . . . 100
Coffeetime Breads and
    Rolls Chapter . . . 64-102
Cornbreads
    Maryland Cornbread . . . 106
    Southern Bacon
      Brunchers . . . 114
    Spicy Raisin Cornbread . . . 122

Corned Beef
    Cheeza Corned Beef . . . 133
    Corned Beef Rye Twist . . . 127
Cornmeal
    Chunk O'Cheese Bread . . . 37
    Maryland Cornbread . . . 106
    Southern Bacon
      Brunchers . . . 114
    Southern Cornmeal Rolls . . . 49
    Spicy Raisin Cornbread . . . 122
    Three-Way Dinner Rolls . . . 44
Country Company Rolls . . . 49
Country Garden
    Casserole Bread . . . 36
Country Kitchen
    Doughnuts . . . 119
County Fair Egg Bread . . . 32
Cranberry
    Cranberry Crisscross
      Coffee Cake . . . 112
    Holiday Cranberry Bread . . . 121
Crescents . . . 40
Crunchy Cream-Filled
    Kuchen . . . 77
Crusty Dinner Rolls . . . 43
Crusty French Bread . . . 30

d

Danish Butter Rolls . . . 81
Danish Coffee Cake, Rich . . . 76
Danish Krispies, Orange . . . 97
Danish Kuchen, Royal . . . 107
Dark Orange Raisin Bread . . . 35
Date
    Blind Date Surprise Rolls . . . 96
    Date-Rich Bran Bread . . . 110
    Up-To-Date Bread . . . 26
Deviled Snack Bread . . . 130
Dice O'Derv . . . 128
Dilly Casserole Bread . . . 56
Dinner and Luncheon
    Rolls Chapter . . . 38-54
Directions . . . 8
Double Butterscotch
    Crescents . . . 86
Double Trick Cheese Bread . . . 138
Doughboys . . . 97

Doughnuts
   Cinnamon Whirl
      Doughnuts . . . 100
   Coffee-Time Doughnuts . . . 100
   Country Kitchen
      Doughnuts . . . 119
   Doughboys . . . 97
Dried Beef
   Country Garden
      Casserole Bread . . . 36
   Dice O'Derv . . . 128

e

Easy Cheesy Buns . . . 61
Easy Prune Loaf . . . 109
Egg Bread, County Fair . . . 32
Eggs, All About . . . 6
English Honey Loaf . . . 109
English Oatwheels . . . 99
Equivalents . . . 10
European Coffee Cake . . . 79

f

Fan-Tans . . . 40
Festive Olive Spread . . . 14
Finger Rolls . . . 40
Flaky Butter Brioche . . . 48
Flour, All About . . . 4
French Breads
   Crusty French Bread . . . 30
   French Boy Loaf . . . 127
   French Bread Braids . . . 30
   French Onion Bread . . . 32
   Golden-Crust Bread . . . 31
Frosting Mix
   Apricot Dandies . . . 94
   Lemon Twist Treat . . . 72
   Nutty Buttercups . . . 86
Frostings and Glazes . . . 12
Frosty Cinnamon Twisters . . . 84

g

Garlic Cheese Toast . . . 28
Golden Cake Bread . . . 61
Golden Cheesies . . . 132
Golden-Crust Bread . . . 31
Golden Onion Rolls . . . 47

Graham Cracker
   Brown Bread . . . 109

h

Half-Time Spoon Rolls . . . 62
Ham
   Ham Chutney Canapés . . . 134
   Ham 'N Tater Pom Poms . . . 139
   Ham Sensations . . . 138
Hard Sauce . . . 14
Hattie's Garden Crescents . . . 49
Hawaiian Coffee Ring . . . 76
Herb and Butter Bread . . . 34
Herb Loaf, Butterflake . . . 34
Herb Stickles . . . 52
High Altitude Adjustments . . . 7
Holiday
   Can-Pan Fruit Bread . . . 29
   Holiday Cranberry Bread . . . 121
   Holiday Treat . . . 123
   Jiffy Mince Coffee Ring . . . 107
   Merry-Go-Round
      Coffee Cake . . . 66
   Mince Crowned Muffins . . . 119
   No-Knead Holiday Bread . . . 58
   Raised Holiday Muffins . . . 62
   Snow Ring . . . 80
Honey
   English Honey Loaf . . . 109
   Honey Ambrosia
      Coffee Cake . . . 113
   Honey Butter . . . 14
   Honey Crust Whirligigs . . . 47
   Honey Fingers . . . 85
   Honey Twin Rolls . . . 60
   Honey-Wheat Bread . . . 26
   Yam-Yam Honey Buns . . . 98
Hot Roll Mix
   Apricot Dandies . . . 94
   Barbecue Twists . . . 53
   Cherry Ring . . . 67
   Cinnamon Nut Crisps . . . 98
   Crunchy Cream-Filled
      Kuchen . . . 77
   Fan-Tasties . . . 95
   Hattie's Garden Crescents . . . 49
   Honey Fingers . . . 85

Lemon Nut Rolls . . . 93
Nutty Buttercups . . . 86
Peanut Glazed Rolls . . . 89
Sunflower Coffee Cake . . . 75
Sweet Petals . . . 66
Sweet Posies . . . 94
Hot Tuna Dip . . . 126

i

Ingredients . . . 9
Italian Supper Loaf . . . 134

j

Jam-Dandy Muffins . . . 116
Jiffy Mince Coffee Ring . . . 107

k

Kuchen, Kwik Peach . . . 115
Kuchen, Royal Danish . . . 107
Kwik Peach Kuchen . . . 115

l

Lemon Frosting or Glaze . . . 12
Lemon Nut Rolls . . . 93
Lemon Twist Treat . . . 72
Limpa Muffins, Swedish . . . 123
Liquid, All About . . . 6
Little Miss Muffins . . . 119
Lucky Lemon Clovers . . . 91
Luncheon Meat
   Deviled Snack Bread . . . 130
   French Boy Loaf . . . 127

m

Mandarin Coffee Cake . . . 112
Maple
   Maple Butter Twists . . . 67
   Maple Frosting or Glaze . . . 12
   Maple-Nut
      Cinnamon Rolls . . . 82
Marmalade Twist . . . 70
Maryland Cornbread . . . 106
Measurements . . . 10
Measures . . . 10, 11
Meat Balls A Go-Go . . . 129
Menu Planning . . . 7
Merry-Go-Round
   Coffee Cake . . . 66

Merry Mince Brown Bread . . . 113
Mincemeat
   Cinnaminco Cider Buns . . . 95
   Jiffy Mince Coffee Ring . . . 107
   Mince Crowned Muffins . . . 119
   Merry Mince
      Brown Bread . . . 113
Mocha Frosting or Glaze . . . 12
Muffin Mix Buffet Bread . . . 36
Muffins
   Blueberry Brunch Loaf . . . 104
   English Oatwheels . . . 99
   Jam-Dandy Muffins . . . 116
   Little Miss Muffins . . . 119
   Mince Crowned Muffins . . . 119
   Orange Streusel Muffins . . . 117
   Raised Holiday Muffins . . . 62
   Spicy Apple Crunch Cake . . . 106
   Swedish Limpa Muffins . . . 123

n

New Method of
   Bread Making . . . 16-19
No-Knead Breads
   Apricot Dandies . . . 94
   Barbecue Twists . . . 53
   Beauty Bow Coffee Cakes . . . 71
   Blind Date Surprise Rolls . . . 96
   Buttercrust Flake-Aparts . . . 45
   Caraway Bran Bread . . . 27
   Cherry Ring . . . 67
   Cinnamince Cider Buns . . . 95
   Cinnamon Nut Crisps . . . 98
   Coffee-Time Doughnuts . . . 100
   Country Company Rolls . . . 49
   Deviled Snack Bread . . . 130
   Double Butterscotch
      Crescents . . . 86
   Doughboys . . . 97
   English Oatwheels . . . 99
   European Coffeecake . . . 79
   Fan-Tasties . . . 95
   French Boy Loaf . . . 127
   Hattie's Garden Crescents . . . 49
   Herb Stickles . . . 52
   Honey Fingers . . . 85
   Lemon Nut Rolls . . . 93

Lemon Twist Treat . . . 72
Maple Butter Twists . . . 67
Maple-Nut
   Cinnamon Rolls . . . 82
Marmalade Twist . . . 70
No-Knead Holiday Bread . . . 58
Nutty Buttercups . . . 86
Old-Fashioned Nut Loaf . . . 81
Old Plantation Rolls . . . 42
Olive Polka-Dot Bread . . . 128
Orange Blossom
   Coffee Cake . . . 74
Orange Butter
   Coffee Cake . . . 74
Parmesan Honor Rolls . . . 46
Peanut Glazed Rolls . . . 89
Quick Praline Rolls . . . 84
Ring-A-Lings . . . 87
Snow Ring . . . 80
Sunflower Coffeecake . . . 75
Swedish Ripple
   Coffee Cake . . . 79
Sweet Posies . . . 94
Table Talk Rolls . . . 42
Three-Way Dinner Rolls . . . 44
Topsy-Turvy Coffee Ring . . . 77
Vichyssoise Feather Fans . . . 44
Yam-Yam Honey Buns . . . 98
Nut Bread Loaves
   Aloha Banana Bread . . . 110
   Banana Luncheon Bread . . . 111
   Blueberry Brunch Loaf . . . 104
   Easy Prune Loaf . . . 109
   English Honey Loaf . . . 109
   Holiday Cranberry Bread . . . 121
   Holiday Treat . . . 123
   Nutty Apricot Snack Loaf . . . 122
   Old Country Raisin Loaf . . . 114
   Peachy Nut Bread . . . 110
   Pennsylvania
      Applesauce Bread . . . 114
   Peppy Apple-Cheese
      Bread . . . 108
   Pumpkin Tea Loaf . . . 120
Nut Loaf, Old-Fashioned . . . 81
Nutty Apricot Snack Loaf . . . 122
Nutty Buttercups . . . 86

Pennsylvania
   Applesauce Bread . . . 114
Peppy Apple-Cheese
   Bread . . . 108
Pineapple
   Cinnamon Pine-Rolls . . . 93
   Honey Ambrosia
      Coffee Cake . . . 113
   Pineapple Raisin Tea Ring . . . 75
   Pineapple Supreme Rolls . . . 91

O

Old Country Raisin Loaf . . . 114
Old-Fashioned Nut Loaf . . . 81
Old Plantation Rolls . . . 42
Olive Cheese Nuggets . . . 129
Olive Polka-Dot Bread . . . 128
Onion
   Barbecue Twists . . . 53
   French Onion Bread . . . 32
   Golden Onion Rolls . . . 47
   Ham Sensations . . . 138
   Onion Patch Pudding. . . 117
   Onion Rye Rolls . . . 52
   Savory Snacks . . . 138
Orange
   Almond Marmalettes . . . 59
   Cinnamon Swirl
      Orange Loaf . . . 80
   Dark Orange Raisin Bread . . . 35
   Fan-Tasties . . . 95
   Fluffy Orange Spread . . . 15
   Mandarin Coffee Cake . . . 112
   Marmalade Twist . . . 70
   Nutty Apricot Snack Loaf . . . 122
   Orange Blosson
      Coffee Cake . . . 74
   Orange Butter
      Coffee Cake . . . 74
   Orange Danish Krispies . . . 97
   Orange Frosting or Glaze . . . 12
   Orange Glory Rolls . . . 90
   Orange Streusel Muffins . . . 117
   Ring-A-Lings . . . 87

p

Pan Rolls . . . 40
Parkerhouse Easy's . . . 42
Parkerhouse Rolls, Quick . . . 41
Parmesan Honor Rolls . . . 46
Peach
   Kwik Peach Kuchen . . . 115
   Peach Flip . . . 70
   Peachy Nut Bread . . . 110
Peanut Butter
     Bread 'N Rolls . . . 27
Peanut Butter Brunch Cake . . . 113
Peanut Glazed Rolls . . . 89
Pecan Sunrise Bread . . . 107
Pizza
   Cheeza Corned Beef . . . 133
   Pizza Dippers . . . 130
   Pizza Sauce . . . 130
Popover Puffs, Cheese . . . 118
Porch Supper Braids . . . 53
Praline Rolls, Quick . . . 84
Proofing, All About . . . 7
Prune
   Easy Prune Loaf . . . 109
   Prune Bran Loaf . . . 35
Pumpkin Tea Loaf . . . 123

q

Quick Breads Chapter . . . 102-124
Quick Praline Rolls . . . 84

r

Raised Holiday Muffins . . . 62
Raisin
   Apple Country
     Coffee Cake . . . 68
   Dark Orange Raisin Bread . . . 35
   Holiday Treat . . . 120
   Old Country Raisin Loaf . . . 114
   Pineapple Raisin
     Tea Ring . . . 75
   Raisin Apple Pair . . . 68
   Royal Danish Kuchen . . . 107
   Spicy Raisin Corn Bread . . . 122
Refrigerated Biscuits
   Cinnamon Nut Crisps . . . 98

Ham-Chutney Canapés . . . 134
Sweet Posies . . . 94
Refrigerated Crescent Rolls
   Coconut Butter Pastries . . . 92
   Honey Ambrosia
     Coffee Cake . . . 113
   Parmesan Honor Rolls . . . 46
   Sausage Snacks . . . 138
Rich Danish Coffee Cake . . . 76
Ring-A-Lings . . . 87
Rolls, Crispy Yeast
   Butter Crispies . . . 99
   Cinnamon Nut Crisps . . . 98
   Danish Butter Rolls . . . 81
   Orange Danish Krispies . . . 97
   Quick Praline Rolls . . . 84
Rolls, Dinner
   Barbecue Twist . . . 53
   Butter-Flake Rolls . . . 43
   Buttercrust Flake-Aparts . . . 45
   Clover Cheese Rolls . . . 46
   Country Company Rolls . . . 49
   Crusty Dinner Rolls . . . 43
   Easy Cheesy Buns . . . 61
   Flaky Butter Brioche . . . 48
   Golden Onion Rolls . . . 47
   Half-Time Spoon Rolls . . . 62
   Hattie's Garden Crescents . . . 49
   Honey Crust Whirligigs . . . 47
   Honey Twin Rolls . . . 60
   Old Plantation Rolls . . . 42
   Onion Rye Rolls . . . 52
   Parkerhouse Easy's . . . 42
   Parmesan Honor Rolls . . . 46
   Peanut Butter
     Bread 'N Rolls . . . 27
   Porch Supper Braids . . . 53
   Savory Spoon Buns . . . 61
   Smoky Barbecue Buns . . . 50
   Sophie's Flaky
     French Crescents . . . 87
   Southern Cornmeal Rolls . . . 49
   Table Talk Rolls . . . 42
   Tato-Flake Cheese Buns . . . 59
   Three-Way Dinner Rolls . . . 44
   Vichyssoise Feather Fans . . . 44
Rolls, Sweet
   Almond Rolls . . . 90
   Apricot Dandies . . . 94

Blind Date
   Surprise Rolls . . . 96
Butter Crispies . . . 99
Butter-Nut Swirls . . . 88
Butterflier "8's" . . . 83
Buttery Caramel Quicks . . . 123
Cinnamince Cider Buns . . . 95
Cinnamon Nut Crisps . . . 98
Cinnamon Pine-Rolls . . . 93
Cinnamon Whirl
   Doughnuts . . . 100
Coconut Butter Pastries . . . 92
Coffee-Time
   Cinnamon Rolls . . . 83
Coffee-Time Doughnuts . . . 100
Danish Butter Rolls . . . 81
Double Butterscotch
   Crescents . . . 86
Doughboys . . . 97
Fan-Tasties . . . 95
Frosty Cinnamon
   Twisters . . . 84
Honey Fingers . . . 85
Lemon Nut Rolls . . . 93
Lucky Lemon Clovers . . . 91
Maple-Nut
   Cinnamon Rolls . . . 82
Nutty Buttercups . . . 86
Orange Danish Krispies . . . 97
Orange Glory Rolls . . . 90
Peanut Glazed Rolls . . . 89
Pineapple Supreme Rolls . . . 91
Quick Praline Rolls . . . 84
Raised Holiday Muffins . . . 62
Ring-A-Lings . . . 87
Sophie's Flaky
   French Crescents . . . 87
Sunny-Side-Up Rolls . . . 96
Sweet Posies . . . 94
Two-Way Coffee Bread . . . 58
Whole Wheat
   Caramel Rolls . . . 85
Yam-Yam Honey Buns . . . 98
Royal Danish Kuchen . . . 107
Rum Frosting or Glaze . . . 12
Rye
   Bit O'Rye Breadsticks . . . 53
   Cheese Roll Loaf . . . 37
   Corned Beef Rye Twist . . . 127

Dark Orange Raisin Bread . . . 35
Onion Rye Rolls . . . 52
Scandinavian Rye Bread . . . 25
Swedish Limpa Muffins . . . 123

S

Salt, All About . . . 6
Sausage Snacks . . . 135
Savory Snacks . . . 138
Savory Spoon Buns . . . 61
Scandinavian Rye Bread . . . 25
Shaping A Loaf . . . 22, 23
Shaping Rolls . . . 40, 41
Shortening, All About . . . 6
Shrimp Bubbles . . . 134
Smoky Barbecue Buns . . . 50
Snack Breads
    Cheese-Crusted
      Flat Bread . . . 126
    Cheese Snack Bread . . . 128
    Cheeza Corned Beef . . . 133
    Corned Beef Rye Twist . . . 127
    Deviled Snack Bread . . . 130
    Double Trick
      Cheese Bread . . . 138
    French Boy Loaf . . . 127
    Olive Polka-Dot Bread . . . 128
    Soup and Sandwich
      Bread . . . 136
Snackeroons . . . 139
Snacks
    Beach Balls . . . 129
    Bleu Cheese Puffs . . . 139
    Cheese Caraway Nips . . . 135
    Cheese Nibblers . . . 135
    Cheese Secrets . . . 132
    Dice O'Derv . . . 128
    Golden Cheesies . . . 132
    Ham Chutney Canapés . . . 134
    Ham 'N Tater Pom Poms . . . 139
    Ham Sensations . . . 138
    Meat Balls A Go-Go . . . 129
    Olive Cheese Nuggets . . . 129
    Pizza Dippers . . . 130
    Sausage Snacks . . . 135
    Savory Snacks . . . 138
    Shrimp Bubbles . . . 134
    Snackeroons . . . 139

Southern Bacon
    Brunchers . . . 114
    Tidbit Toppers . . . 132
    Tuna-Tater Thins . . . 126
    Tuna Teasers . . . 135
Snacks Chapter . . . 124-140
Snow Ring . . . 80
Sophie's Flaky
    French Crescents . . . 87
Soup and Sandwich Bread . . . 136
Southern Bacon Brunchers . . . 114
Southern Cornmeal Rolls . . . 49
Spice Frosting or Glaze . . . 12
Spicy Apple Crunch Cake . . . 106
Spicy Raisin Corn Bread . . . 122
Spreads . . . 14
Storage of Breads . . . 7
Substitutions . . . 11
Sugar, All About . . . 6
Sugar Mountain Loaf . . . 60
Sunflower Coffee Cake . . . 75
Sunny-Side-Up Rolls . . . 96
Supper Loaf, Italian . . . 134
Swedish Limpa Muffins . . 123
Swedish Ripple
    Coffee Cake . . . 79
Sweet Petals . . . 66
Sweet Posies . . . 94
Sweetheart Coffee Cake . . . 78

t

Table Talk Rolls . . . 42
Tato-Flake Cheese Buns . . . 59
Terms . . . 8, 9
Three-Way Dinner Rolls . . . 44
Tidbit Toppers . . . 132
Topsy-Turvy Coffee Ring . . . 77
Tuna Dip, Hot . . . 126
Tuna-Tater Thins . . . 126
Tuna Teasers . . . 135
Two-Tone Loaves . . . 31
Two-Way Coffee Bread . . . 58

u

Up-To-Date Bread . . . 26

V

Vanilla Frosting or Glaze . . . 12
Vichyssoise Feather Fans . . . 44

W

Whipped Butter . . . 14
Whole Wheat
    Honey-Wheat Bread . . . 26
    Three-Way Dinner Rolls . . . 44
    Two-Tone Loaves . . . 31
    Whole Wheat
      Caramel Rolls . . . 85

y

Yam-Yam Honey Buns . . . 98
Yeast, All About . . . 5
Yeast Bread Loaves
    Butterflake Herb Loaf . . . 34
    Can-Pan Fruit Bread . . . 29
    Caraway Bran Bread . . . 27
    Cheese Roll Loaf . . . 37
    Chunk O'Cheese Bread . . . 37
    Cinnamon Swirl
      Orange Loaf . . . 80
    Country Garden
      Casserole Bread . . . 36
    County Fair Egg Bread . . . 32
    Crusty French Bread . . . 30
    Dark Orange
      Raisin Bread . . . 35
    Dilly Casserole Bread . . . 56
    French Bread Braids . . . 30
    French Onion Bread . . . 32
    Garlic Cheese Toast . . . 28
    Golden Cake Bread . . . 61
    Golden-Crust Bread . . . 31
    Herb and Butter Bread . . . 34
    Honey-Wheat Bread . . . 26
    Muffin Mix Buffet Bread . . . 36
    No-Knead Holiday Bread . . . 58
    Old-Fashioned Nut Loaf . . . 81
    Peanut Butter
      Bread 'N Rolls . . . 27
    Prune Bran Loaf . . . 35
    Scandinavian Rye Bread . . . 25
    Two-Tone Loaves . . . 31
    Up-To-Date Bread . . . 26
Yeast Breads Chapter . . . 20-38